Culture of the Jews
101 Notable Jewish Cultural Traditions

© **Copyright 2023 - All rights reserved.**

The content contained within this book may not be reproduced, duplicated, or transmitted without direct written permission from the author or the publisher.

Under no circumstances will any blame or legal responsibility be held against the publisher or author for any damages, reparation, or monetary loss due to the information contained within this book, either directly or indirectly.

Legal Notice:

This book is copyright-protected. It is only for personal use. You cannot amend, distribute, sell, use, quote, or paraphrase any part of the content within this book without the consent of the author or publisher.

Disclaimer Notice:

Please note the information contained within this document is for educational and entertainment purposes only. All effort has been executed to present accurate, up-to-date, reliable, and complete information. No warranties of any kind are declared or implied. Readers acknowledge that the author is not engaging in the rendering of legal, financial, medical, or professional advice. The content within this book has been derived from various sources. Please consult a licensed professional before attempting any techniques outlined in this book.

By reading this document, the reader agrees that under no circumstances is the author responsible for any losses, direct or indirect, that are incurred as a result of the use of the information contained within this document, including, but not limited to, errors, omissions, or inaccuracies.

Table of Contents

INTRODUCTION 1
CHAPTER 1: SHABBAT AND HOLY TRADITIONS 3
CHAPTER 2: THE WHEEL OF LIFE 19
CHAPTER 3: FEAST DAYS AND FAST DAYS 33
CHAPTER 4: THE POWER OF PRAYER 49
CHAPTER 5: SYMBOLS AND SACRED OBJECTS 63
CHAPTER 6: MUSICAL TRADITIONS 78
CHAPTER 7: HOME AND FAMILY TRADITION 92
CHAPTER 8: LEARNING, WISDOM, AND ACADEMIA 108
CHAPTER 9: ART AND CREATIVITY 123
CHAPTER 10: THE CULTURE OF THE JEWISH DIASPORA 136
CONCLUSION 146
GLOSSARY OF TERMS 149
REFERENCES 153

Introduction

In a world of constant change, where traditions sometimes fade into obscurity, there is something profoundly enriching about connecting with the past. Think about embracing the heritage that has shaped cultures and communities over centuries. Through this connection, you find meaning, a sense of continuity, and a plethora of stories that resonate across time. It's the essence of "Culture of the Jews - 101 Notable Jewish Cultural Traditions."

This book is a gateway to the world of Jewish culture, traditions, and rituals. It's an opportunity to embark on a journey that unveils the very heart of a vibrant and enduring heritage. You may wonder, why should I delve into history and tradition? Within history lies a treasure trove of wisdom, identity, and insight that can enrich your life in unexpected ways. By delving into the past, you better understand the present. In doing so, you shape a more informed and enlightened future.

A Comprehensive Guide to Jewish Heritage

Culture of the Jews is a comprehensive guide with a holistic view of Jewish heritage. Whether new to the subject or seeking to deepen your understanding, this book is crafted with your needs in mind. It's a compass that navigates through the intricacies of Judaism, offering you a roadmap to explore the various facets that define its essence.

Accessible and Engaging

One of the defining features of the Culture of the Jews is its accessibility. Complex concepts are presented in a manner that's easy to understand without sacrificing the depth and authenticity that the subject deserves. This book is your companion, guiding you through a world of tradition, symbolism, and celebration. It's perfect for beginners and those eager to reconnect with their roots.

Everything You Need, All in One Place

In a sea of information, it can be overwhelming to piece together the puzzle of a culture's heritage. *Culture of the Jews* solves this challenge by encompassing everything you need to know about Jewish tradition within its pages. From the sacred observances of Shabbat to the cultural influences of the Jewish diaspora, this book is a comprehensive resource that leaves no stone unturned.

The Power of Understanding

Why is understanding history and tradition so important? As you explore Jewish culture's stories, customs, and rituals, you unlock a deeper appreciation for the narratives that have shaped societies for generations. You gain insight into the values that have guided communities through challenges and triumphs and discover the common threads that weave humanity together.

Unique Insights for Modern Times

While this book takes you on a journey through history, it also presents insights that resonate with the complexities of the modern world. The relevance of tradition in your fast-paced life becomes apparent as you recognize how ancient wisdom can offer guidance and a sense of belonging amid change.

By delving into the depths of Jewish culture, you'll gain knowledge and open your heart to the stories of generations past that continue to resonate with meaning and purpose. It's time to explore the rituals that shape Jewish life, uncover the symbols that carry profound meanings, and discover the melodies that have echoed through the ages. As you journey through these chapters, may you find inspiration, connection, and a renewed appreciation for the treasures that heritage brings. Your adventure awaits!

Chapter 1: Shabbat and Holy Traditions

In the gentle embrace of Friday evening, Jewish households worldwide undergo a transformative shift. The ordinary becomes sacred, the mundane is elevated, and the hurried pace of modern life gives way to the serene, cherished tradition of Shabbat.

These rituals, spanning millennia, are not merely acts of faith. They are threads weaving the fabric of Jewish identity.

The Weekly Sanctuary: Shabbat (a Day of Rest)

Few Jewish holy traditions are as vibrant and enduring as Shabbat. It's the sacred oasis that arrives at the end of each week. Rooted in ancient history and infused with timeless significance, Shabbat is a beacon of rest, reflection, and renewal in the Jewish calendar.

Historical Origins

To truly appreciate the beauty of Shabbat, you must journey back to its origins. The story begins with the Book of Genesis, where God rested on the seventh day after six days of creation. This Divine act of rest established a blueprint for humanity. One day in seven is dedicated to replenishing the spirit and nurturing the soul.

Shabbat, often called the "Sabbath," commemorates God's rest and serves as a tangible connection to the Divine. It is a day when Jews are commanded to cease work, a symbolic act of imitating God's creative pause. But Shabbat is more than a weekly respite. It's a profound affirmation of Jewish identity, a day to bask in the joys of family, community, and spiritual reflection.

Observance Practices

Jewish households welcome Shabbat by lighting candles.
Olaf.herfurth, CC BY-SA 3.0 <https://creativecommons.org/licenses/by-sa/3.0>, via Wikimedia Commons: https://commons.wikimedia.org/wiki/File:Shabbat_Candles.jpg

The observance of Shabbat begins at sunset on Friday and concludes at nightfall on Saturday, spanning approximately twenty-five hours. During this sacred interlude, a series of customs and rituals unfold, each laden with symbolic significance:

- **Candle Lighting:** Jewish households welcome Shabbat by lighting candles as the sun dips below the horizon. This act signifies the transition from the mundane to the sacred, infusing the home with warmth and spirituality.

- **Kiddush:** The evening meal on Friday commences with Kiddush, a blessing over wine or grape juice. It sanctifies the day and reminds participants of the sacred bond between the Jewish people and God.

- **Challah:** A special braided bread, challah, graces the Shabbat table. Before eating, a blessing is recited, acknowledging the sustenance provided by the Creator.

- **Rest from Work:** Shabbat is a day of complete rest, and traditional Jewish law prohibits engaging in activities that fall under the category of work. This cessation of labor fosters a sense of tranquility and mindfulness by refocusing the mind on the Divine.
- **Synagogue Services:** Jews gather in synagogues for prayers and communal worship on Friday evening and Saturday morning. These services are a communal expression of devotion and unity.
- **Shabbat Meals:** The Friday night and Saturday afternoon meals are central to Shabbat observance. These gatherings with family and friends are infused with blessings, songs, and a festive atmosphere.
- **Havdalah:** As Shabbat draws to a close, a ceremony called Havdalah is performed. It involves lighting a unique multi-wicked candle, smelling spices, and reciting blessings. Havdalah marks the separation between the holy rest day and the workweek ahead.

The Profound Impact

Shabbat isn't just a day of physical rest but a spiritual pause. It's a chance to recharge the soul's batteries. It's a weekly reminder of what truly matters in life: connection, gratitude, and reverence for the Divine. Through Shabbat, Jewish tradition teaches the importance of balance, reminding us that even in the busiest of lives, there must be moments of respite and reflection. In a world marked by constant motion, Shabbat is when families gather, prayers rise, and the spirit finds solace. It's a tradition transcending generations, connecting Jews across time and space to a shared heritage and a sacred rhythm of life.

Rosh Hashanah: Embracing a New Year with Tradition

Rosh Hashanah, the Jewish New Year, beckons with its blend of history and modern relevance. Rooted in ancient customs, it is cherished in Jewish life today.

Historical Origins

Originating in antiquity, Rosh Hashanah signifies a time of judgment and introspection. It marks the opening of the "Book of Life" and the ten days leading to Yom Kippur, the Day of Atonement.

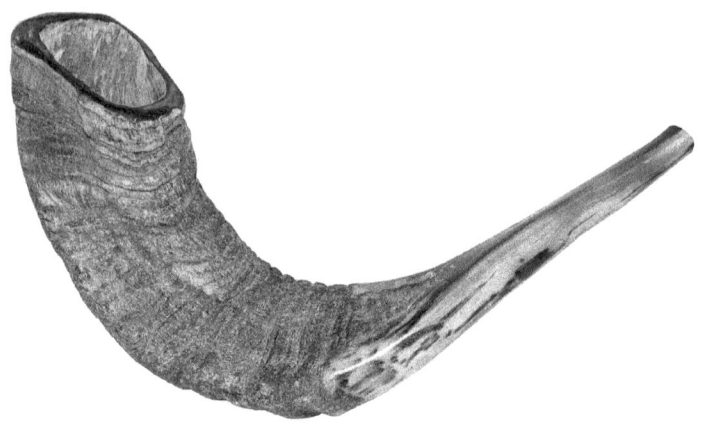

The blowing of the shofar ushers in Rosh Hashanah.
Zachi Evenor, CC BY-SA 4.0 <https://creativecommons.org/licenses/by-sa/4.0>, via Wikimedia Commons: https://commons.wikimedia.org/wiki/File:Shofar-16-Zachi-Evenor.jpg

Observance Practices

- **Shofar Blowing:** The resonant call of the shofar, a ram's horn trumpet, ushers in the holiday, inspiring reflection and repentance.
- **Tashlich:** Symbolically casting away sins into flowing water, Tashlich embodies the desire for a fresh start.
- **Festive Meals:** Rosh Hashanah feasts feature symbolic foods like apples and honey, representing a sweet year ahead.
- **Prayer and Synagogue Services:** Jews gather to recite special Rosh Hashanah prayers, acknowledging God's role as Judge and King.
- **Personal Reflection:** The holiday prompts introspection, forgiveness-seeking, and goal-setting.

Tying into Modern Jewish Life

Rosh Hashanah's timeless message transcends history. It fosters family bonds, like Sara's, who shares, *"It's about cherishing connections and setting intentions for the year ahead."*

Rosh Hashanah resonates in this fast-paced world, offering moments of reflection and connection. It embodies the enduring relevance of tradition, inspiring renewal and hope. In essence, Rosh Hashanah reminds you that history lives within people. Ancient customs shape your life, and personal growth and meaningful connections remain timeless.

Yom Kippur: The Day of Atonement

In the mosaic of Jewish holidays, Yom Kippur stands out as a day of deep introspection, atonement, and transformation. This solemn day, known as the Day of Atonement, carries a rich historical legacy and holds profound significance in modern Jewish life.

Historical Origins

Yom Kippur finds its roots in ancient times. It is the culmination of the Ten Days of Repentance, beginning with Rosh Hashanah. The Torah designates Yom Kippur as a day of fasting, prayer, and spiritual reflection. Historically, it recalls the High Priest's entry into the Holy of Holies in the ancient Temple to seek forgiveness for the people's sins.

Observance Practices

The observance of Yom Kippur is marked by a series of practices aimed at deep introspection and reconciliation:

- **Fasting:** Yom Kippur is a day of complete fasting, abstaining from food and drink for approximately twenty-five hours. This physical act symbolizes purification and a focus on the soul.

- **Prayer and Synagogue Services:** Jews gather for lengthy synagogue services featuring special prayers and confessions, including the Vidui, where sins are acknowledged.

- **Reflection and Repentance:** Yom Kippur prompts individuals to engage in profound introspection. It is a time to seek forgiveness from God and fellow humans, mending relationships and seeking reconciliation.

- **White Attire:** Many Jews wear white clothing on Yom Kippur, symbolizing purity and a fresh start.

- **Ne'ilah Service:** The concluding service of Yom Kippur, Ne'ilah, carries a sense of urgency, representing the final opportunity for repentance.

Tying into Modern Jewish Life

With its timeless call for self-examination and atonement, Yom Kippur invites individuals to reflect on their actions, seek forgiveness, and embrace the possibility of renewal. It reminds followers that inner peace is a path with universal significance. As you observe Yom Kippur, you engage in a profound tradition that bridges the past and the present, offering hope for a more compassionate and self-aware future.

Sukkot: The Feast of Tabernacles

Among various Jewish celebrations, Sukkot shines as a radiant festival known as the Feast of Tabernacles. Rooted in history and infused with symbolism, Sukkot bridges the ancient and modern worlds with a celebration of unity, gratitude, and the joy of harvest.

Historical Origins

Sukkot traces its origins to biblical times, commemorating the journey of the Israelites through the wilderness. It serves as a reminder of the temporary dwellings, or Sukkot, that the Israelites lived in during their wanderings. The holiday also coincides with the harvest season in ancient Israel, making it a time of thanksgiving for the bounties of the land.

Observance Practices

The Sukkah is built when Sukkot is observed.
Rhododendrites, CC BY-SA 4.0 <https://creativecommons.org/licenses/by-sa/4.0>, via Wikimedia Commons: https://commons.wikimedia.org/wiki/File:Sukkah_at_Congregation_Emanu-El_(05326p).jpg

A delightful array of customs and rituals marks the observance of Sukkot:

- **Building the Sukkah**: A central element of Sukkot is the construction of a sukkah, a temporary, open-roofed shelter. Families and communities come together to build and decorate the sukkot, often adorned with fruit, foliage, and decorations.
- **Lulav and Etrog**: During Sukkot, Jews wave a lulav (a bundle of palm, myrtle, and willow branches) and an etrog (a citron fruit) in six directions to symbolize God's presence everywhere.
- **Festive Meals**: Sukkot is celebrated with joyous meals in the sukkah, reminding participants of the harvest season's blessings. It is customary to invite guests, even welcoming the biblical figures of Abraham, Isaac, and Jacob as symbolic guests, known as Ushpizin.
- **Hoshanah Rabbah**: On the seventh day of Sukkot, Jews perform a unique ritual called Hoshanah Rabbah, where they circle the synagogue with the lulav and etrog, seeking Divine blessings.

Tying into Modern Jewish Life

Sukkot transcends its historical roots, embodying a timeless message of gratitude, community, and humility. In today's world, Sukkot is a meaningful reminder of the importance of appreciating life's transient joys and fostering unity. It encourages individuals and families to pause, spend time outdoors, and acknowledge the impermanence of our material possessions.

A young mother, Rachel, shares, "*Sukkot has become a beautiful tradition for our family. We gather in the sukkah, under the open sky, sharing meals, stories, and laughter. It's a reminder of our connection to nature and the importance of embracing the temporary.*"

Hanukkah: A Festival of Lights

Hanukkah, or the Festival of Lights, is a Jewish holiday with a rich historical backdrop. It commemorates the miraculous events when the Jewish people, under the Maccabean leadership, reclaimed the Holy Temple in Jerusalem from the Greek-Syrian oppressors. This momentous victory marked the end of religious persecution and a return to Jewish sovereignty in their homeland.

Historical Origins

Hanukkah's origins are traced back to a tumultuous period in Jewish history. In the 2nd century BCE, Israel was under the rule of the Seleucid

Empire, which sought to suppress Jewish customs and impose Hellenistic culture. A small band of Jewish rebels, led by Judah Maccabee, rose against the oppressors and, against all odds, reclaimed the Holy Temple in Jerusalem.

The miracle of Hanukkah, which means "dedication" in Hebrew, occurred during the rededication of the Temple. According to tradition, a single cruse of consecrated olive oil, enough for one day, miraculously burned for eight days until new oil could be prepared. This miracle is celebrated with the lighting of the menorah during Hanukkah.

Observance Practices

The menorah is the centerpiece of Hanukkah.
https://www.pexels.com/photo/gifts-for-hanukkah-4033351/

A luminous array of customs and traditions marks the observance of Hanukkah:

- **Lighting the Menorah:** The centerpiece of Hanukkah is the menorah—a nine-branched candelabrum. One candle is lit each night for eight nights, with a ninth candle, the shamash (servant), which is used to light the others. This ritual symbolizes the increasing light and hope during the holiday.

- **Playing Dreidel:** The dreidel, a spinning top with Hebrew letters, is a traditional Hanukkah game. Players use tokens (often chocolate coins) and spin the dreidel to determine the distribution of the pot.

- **Sufganiyot and Latkes:** Hanukkah is a time for delicious foods like sufganiyot (jelly-filled doughnuts) and latkes (potato pancakes), traditionally fried in oil to commemorate the oil miracle.
- **Gift-Giving:** In some Jewish communities, especially in the diaspora, it's customary to exchange gifts during Hanukkah, akin to the broader cultural practice of gift-giving during the holiday season.

Modern Relevance

In modern Jewish life, Hanukkah is a beacon of hope, resilience, and religious freedom. It's a time for families to unite, strengthen bonds, and instill a sense of identity and pride in their heritage. Beyond its historical significance, Hanukkah's message of spreading light in the darkest times resonates universally, transcending religious boundaries.

As the menorah's glow pierces the winter night, it reminds us of the enduring power of faith, perseverance, and the triumph of good over adversity. Hanukkah is a celebration of not only the past but also a guiding light for the present and future, illuminating the path toward unity and hope for all.

Simchat Torah: Celebrating Torah's Completion and Renewal

Simchat Torah, "Rejoicing in the Torah," is a jubilant Jewish holiday that marks the culmination of the annual Torah reading cycle and the start of a new one. This festive occasion brims with spiritual renewal and energy.

Historical Origins

Simchat Torah's origins trace back to the Babylonian exile when public Torah reading was prohibited. Upon their return to Israel, Jews began reading the entire Torah in a year, evolving into the Simchat Torah celebrated today.

Observance Practices

- **Hakafot (Torah Circles):** Central to Simchat Torah are joyous processions, "hakafot," where Torah scrolls are paraded around the synagogue, accompanied by singing, dancing, flags, and music.

- **Aliyot (Torah Honors):** Congregants are called to the Torah for aliyot, reciting blessings before and after reading a Torah portion, a revered honor.
- **End and Beginning Readings:** Simchat Torah features the reading of the final verses of Deuteronomy followed by the opening verses of Genesis, symbolizing the cyclical nature of Torah study.
- **Singing and Dancing:** The holiday is marked by spirited singing and dancing involving participants of all ages, fostering a sense of community.

Tying into Modern Jewish Life

Simchat Torah retains its significance in modern Jewish life as a reminder of the enduring link between the Jewish people and the Torah. It emphasizes lifelong learning, unity, and celebrating Jewish identity in an ever-changing world. This holiday inspires and unites Jews of diverse backgrounds, reinforcing their shared heritage and values.

Sefirat HaOmer: The Spiritual Journey of Counting

Sefirat HaOmer, the "Counting of the Omer," is a seven-week period in the Jewish calendar that links Passover and Shavuot. During this time, Jews reflect on spiritual growth, traditionally observing partial mourning.

Historical Origins

Sefirat HaOmer gets its name from the biblical command to count the days from the second day of Passover to Shavuot, symbolizing the journey from liberation (Passover) to spiritual enlightenment (Shavuot). Historically, it recalls the preparation of the Jewish people to receive the Torah at Mount Sinai. Spiritually, it's a time for introspection and personal growth, refining character traits, and deepening spiritual awareness.

Observance Practices

- **Counting the Omer:** Every evening, from the second night of Passover until the day before Shavuot, Jews recite a blessing and count the Omer, verbally declaring the day of the count.
- **Partial Mourning:** Traditionally, this period involves partial mourning, restricting activities like weddings and haircuts. Some

also abstain from listening to music.
- **Lag BaOmer:** The 33rd day of the Omer, Lag BaOmer, is a day of celebration marked by bonfires, outings, and weddings.

Tying into Modern Jewish Life

Sefirat HaOmer offers a framework for self-improvement, mindfulness, and character development in today's Jewish life. It reminds individuals that personal growth is a gradual journey requiring daily effort and commitment.

Moreover, it connects two major Jewish holidays, emphasizing the continuity of tradition and the significance of receiving the Torah. This period fosters a reconnection with core values and teachings in a world of distractions.

Sefirat HaOmer invites Jews to embark on an inner journey toward self-improvement, spiritual growth, and a deeper connection to their heritage and faith, encapsulating the timeless wisdom of Jewish tradition.

Lag BaOmer: Igniting Joy Amidst Spiritual Reflection

Lag BaOmer, the 33rd day of the Counting of the Omer, emerges as a radiant celebration within the somber season of Sefirat HaOmer. Jubilant festivities and the illumination of bonfires mark this unique Jewish holiday.

Historical Origins

The name "Lag BaOmer" combines "Lag," signifying the Hebrew letters Lamed (30) and Gimel (3), with "BaOmer," representing the 33rd day of the Omer count. Lag BaOmer finds its roots in Jewish mysticism and the teachings of Rabbi Shimon bar Yochai, a revered sage of the second century CE. Although Rabbi Shimon's passing is observed on this day, it is celebrated as a day of joy because he revealed the mystical Zohar teachings before his demise.

Observance Practices

Bonfires are lit during Lag BaOmer to symbolize the spiritual enlightenment of Rabbi Shimon's teachings.
user:Effib, CC BY-SA 4.0 <https://creativecommons.org/licenses/by-sa/4.0>, via Wikimedia Commons: https://commons.wikimedia.org/wiki/File:Lag_Baomer_Campfires_In_Jerusalem.JPG

- **Bonfires:** Lighting bonfires is a central Lag BaOmer custom, symbolizing the spiritual enlightenment of Rabbi Shimon's teachings. Communities gather around these flames for song, dance, and storytelling.

- **Weddings and Celebrations:** Lag BaOmer temporarily lifts mourning restrictions, allowing for weddings, haircuts, and other joyous events on this day.

- **Pilgrimage to Meron:** Thousands of Jews pilgrimage to Rabbi Shimon's tomb in Meron, Israel, where celebrations include dancing, prayer, and communal gatherings.

Tying into Modern Jewish Life

Lag BaOmer serves as a poignant reminder that moments of joy and celebration can be found even during spiritual reflection. It underscores the depth of Jewish tradition and the importance of passing on mystical teachings. In today's fast-paced world, Lag BaOmer offers a chance for community, unity, and the sharing of ancient wisdom.

This holiday bridges the ancient and the contemporary, embodying the timeless nature of Jewish spirituality. It encourages you to seek moments of light and celebration amidst life's challenges, offering inspiration and unity to Jews worldwide.

Tu B'Av: Jewish Love Day, a Modern Celebration of Affection

Tu B'Av, known as "Jewish Love Day," is a Jewish holiday celebrated on the 15th day of the Hebrew month of Av. Although its origins lie in matchmaking for unmarried women, today, it is often likened to Valentine's Day, a celebration of love and affection.

Historical Origins

Tu B'Av has ancient roots as a day of matchmaking in the times of the Second Temple in Jerusalem. On this day, unmarried women would don white dresses and dance in the vineyards, while young men would come to find potential spouses. It was a joyous occasion symbolizing the search for love and the perpetuation of the Jewish people.

Observance Practices

- **Celebrating Love:** Tu B'Av has evolved into a day to celebrate love in all its forms. Couples express their affection for one another through romantic gestures, such as giving flowers, cards, and special gifts.

- **Outdoor Gatherings:** Similar to its historical roots, some people celebrate outdoors, taking moonlit strolls, having picnics, or even dancing in vineyards.

- **Acts of Kindness:** Many use Tu B'Av to perform acts of kindness, spreading love and positivity within their communities.

Tu B'Av vs. Valentine's Day

While Tu B'Av and Valentine's Day celebrate love, they have distinct historical and cultural backgrounds. Tu B'Av has its roots in Jewish tradition and history, while Valentine's Day is a more secular holiday with Christian origins.

Both holidays, however, emphasize the importance of expressing love and affection to those close to us. In modern times, Tu B'Av is often seen as a day to strengthen romantic relationships and show appreciation for loved ones, aligning it with the spirit of Valentine's Day.

Tu B'Av has evolved from its historical matchmaking origins into a modern celebration of love and affection in the Jewish calendar. It serves as a reminder that love is a universal and timeless bond that transcends cultural boundaries and brings people together.

Yom Hashoah: Honoring the Unforgettable Tragedy

Yom Hashoah, known as Holocaust Remembrance Day, is a solemn day dedicated to remembering the six million Jews who tragically died during the Holocaust.

Historical Origins

Yom Hashoah was established in Israel in 1953 by the Knesset, Israel's parliament, to honor the memory of Holocaust victims. The date chosen for this somber occasion is the 27th day of the Hebrew month of Nisan, which typically falls in April or May. This date was selected as it corresponds with the beginning of the Warsaw Ghetto Uprising in 1943, a symbol of Jewish resistance against the Nazis.

Observance Practices

- **Memorial Ceremonies**: Yom Hashoah is marked by solemn ceremonies in synagogues, schools, and Holocaust memorials. These ceremonies include candle lighting, the recitation of Kaddish (the mourners' prayer), and the reading of names of Holocaust victims.

- **Public Commemorations**: In Israel, a siren sounds, and the entire nation observes a two-minute silence in memory of the victims. Public events, survivor testimonies, and educational programs are held nationwide.

- **Educational Initiatives:** Yom Hashoah is about Holocaust education. Schools and institutions worldwide organize lectures, exhibits, and discussions to ensure that the memory of the Holocaust is passed on to future generations.

Tying into Modern Jewish Life

Yom HaShoah is a solemn reminder of the immense human tragedy that unfolded during the Holocaust. It emphasizes the importance of bearing witness to history, preserving the memory of the victims, and pledging "Never Again." In today's world, where antisemitism and hate crimes persist, Yom HaShoah carries a poignant message about the consequences of intolerance and discrimination.

Yom Ha'atzmaut: Celebrating Israel's Triumph of Independence

Yom Ha'atzmaut, also known as Israeli Independence Day, is a jubilant national holiday commemorating the establishment of the modern State of Israel in 1948. It marks a remarkable moment in Jewish history and serves as a symbol of resilience and determination.

Historical Origins

Yom Ha'atzmaut is celebrated on the 5th day of the Hebrew month of Iyar, corresponding to the Gregorian calendar's May 14th or 15th date. This date represents the culmination of the Zionist movement's efforts and the proclamation of the State of Israel by David Ben-Gurion on May 14, 1948. After nearly two millennia of diaspora, persecution, and longing for a homeland, Jewish people witnessed the rebirth of a sovereign Jewish state in their ancestral land.

Observance Practices

- **Flag-Waving and Parades**: Israeli cities come alive with flag-waving, street parades, and lively celebrations. It's a time of joy and unity as people of all ages participate in the festivities.

- **Fireworks and Concerts**: Spectacular fireworks light up the night skies, and concerts featuring Israeli music and culture are held nationwide.

- **Memorial Ceremonies**: The transition from Yom HaZikaron (Memorial Day) to Yom Ha'atzmaut is marked by a national ceremony at Mount Herzl in Jerusalem. This transition from mourning to celebration is a poignant reminder of the sacrifices made for Israel's existence.

- **Traditional Foods:** Like many Jewish holidays, Yom Ha'atzmaut is celebrated with traditional foods, such as falafel, hummus, and Israeli salads.

Tying into Modern Jewish Life

Yom Ha'atzmaut is a day of pride and solidarity in contemporary Jewish communities. It highlights the importance of supporting and strengthening Israel as a homeland for Jews while also acknowledging the complexities of its modern political and social landscape. It encourages Jewish individuals and communities to engage with Israel in terms of its challenges and achievements, fostering a deeper connection to the Jewish homeland.

Shabbat and the holidays surrounding it are a time of joy and celebration for many Jewish communities worldwide. These important days remind people to reflect on traditions, honor our history, and celebrate the values that bring people together. From Tu B'Av, Yom Hashoah, and Yom Ha'atzmaut to Shabbat itself, these holy days are an integral part of Jewish life and provide meaningful opportunities to connect with the heritage.

Chapter 2: The Wheel of Life

In Jewish tradition, life unfolds through profound and meaningful moments. From birth to adulthood, love, and loss, these milestones are the threads that weave the fabric of Jewish identity and community. From the joyous celebrations of birth and coming of age to the solemn rituals of mourning and remembrance, life is a journey filled with tradition, meaning, and enduring connections.

Brit Milah (Circumcision): A Covenant of Love and Identity

Brit Milah, the ritual circumcision of Jewish boys, is one of Jewish tradition's most fundamental and ancient customs. This sacred ceremony is a testament to the enduring covenant between the Jewish people and the Divine, marking a child's entry into the Jewish community and reaffirming a profound connection to Jewish identity.

Origins and Religious Significance

The roots of Brit Milah trace back to the covenant between God and Abraham, the founding father of Judaism. According to the Book of Genesis, God commanded Abraham to circumcise himself and all males in his household as a sign of the covenant. This act symbolized the Jews' unique relationship with the Divine and their commitment to living a life guided by God's commandments.

Observance Today

Brit Milah is typically held on the eighth day of a male infant's life, a tradition rooted in the Torah. The eighth day is seen as a day of spiritual completeness, and the circumcision is performed by a trained professional called a Mohel.

The ceremony takes place within a loving and supportive community setting. Family and friends gather, creating an atmosphere of unity and joy. A festive meal, known as a Seudat Mitzvah, often follows the ceremony.

The child often wears a miniature kippah on Brit Milah.
H. Pellikka, CC BY-SA 3.0 <http://creativecommons.org/licenses/by-sa/3.0/>, via Wikimedia Commons: https://commons.wikimedia.org/wiki/File:Kipa.jpg

Ceremonial Objects

During the Brit Milah ceremony, several objects hold special significance:

- **Kippah (Yarmulke):** The baby is often dressed in a miniature kippah to symbolize his entry into Jewish life.

- **Kisei Shel Eliyahu (Elijah's Chair):** A special chair is designated for the baby, symbolizing the presence of the Prophet Elijah, who is said to protect infants.

- **Brit Tray:** A tray containing ritual items, such as circumcision instruments and wine, plays a central role in the ceremony.

Prayers and Blessings

The ceremony includes recitation of prayers and blessings, underscoring the significance of the covenant. The Mohel offers prayer and gratitude, and the father often recites the blessing, thanking God for commanding the circumcision.

A Personal Reflection

Ruth, a mother, shares her perspective: "*The Brit Milah of my son was a profoundly emotional moment for our family. It was about more than just a physical act. It was about connecting him to generations of Jews who had walked this path before him.*"

In essence, Brit Milah is a ceremony that transcends the physical act of circumcision. It represents the eternal bond between the Jewish people and their heritage, symbolizing commitment to a life enriched by faith, community, and a profound sense of identity. It is a testament to the enduring strength of Jewish tradition, linking the past, present, and future in a sacred covenant of love and continuity.

Bar/Bat Mitzvah: Coming of Age

The Bar Mitzvah (for boys) and Bat Mitzvah (for girls) represent a profound moment in the life of a Jewish adolescent. These ceremonies mark the transition into adulthood, where young individuals assume responsibility for their faith, actions, and commitment to Jewish tradition.

Origins and Religious Significance

The concept of Bar Mitzvah finds its roots in the Talmud, a central text of Jewish law and tradition. It notes that at age thirteen for boys and twelve for girls, an individual becomes "obligated in commandments." This signifies their newfound spiritual maturity and accountability for their actions.

Observance Today

Bar and Bat Mitzvah ceremonies are celebrated in various ways, but they all share a common thread of joy, spirituality, and community. The heart of these events is the Aliyah, the honor of being called to the Torah during a synagogue service. This act signifies that the young person is now a fully Jewish community member and is responsible for observing Jewish commandments.

Ceremonial Objects

A young person receives their first tallit to symbolize their maturity in faith.
Silar, CC BY-SA 4.0 <https://creativecommons.org/licenses/by-sa/4.0>, via Wikimedia Commons: https://commons.wikimedia.org/wiki/File:02022_0566_Tallit,_Silesia.jpg

- **Tallit (Prayer Shawl):** It is customary for the young person to receive their first tallit, symbolizing their maturity in faith.
- **Siddur (Prayer Book):** Often, the Bar or Bat Mitzvah receives a siddur, a prayer book, as a symbol of their increased involvement in prayer and synagogue life.

Prayers and Readings

The Bar/Bat Mitzvah service often includes an Aliyah to the Torah, during which the child recites a portion of the weekly Torah reading. There may be speeches, reflections on the Torah portion, and blessings. The Haftarah, a reading from the Prophets, is also recited, underscoring the connection between the Torah and the prophetic tradition.

A Personal Reflection

David, a father, reflects on his son's Bar Mitzvah: "Watching my son stand before the congregation, chanting from the Torah, was a moment of immense pride and connection. It was a bridge between generations, a reminder that our tradition lives on through him."

In essence, the Bar and Bat Mitzvah ceremonies symbolize the blossoming of personal identity within the Jewish faith and community. It is a reminder of the enduring legacy of Jewish tradition, where the young generation steps forward to carry the torch of their ancestors.

Jewish Wedding Customs: The Union of Hearts and Heritage

A Jewish wedding is a testament to tradition and love, bringing together centuries-old customs with the promise of a shared future. This sacred ceremony celebrates the union of two individuals and marks the merging of their families and the continuation of Jewish heritage.

Origins and Religious Significance

Jewish wedding customs have deep roots in ancient traditions and religious texts. The sacred union of a man and a woman, called "Kiddushin," is celebrated with great reverence, echoing the Divine partnership between God and the Jewish people.

Observance Today

Modern Jewish weddings blend timeless customs and personal expressions of love. While the specifics can vary among Jewish communities, certain elements are universal.

Ceremonial Objects

- **Ketubah (Marriage Contract):** The Ketubah is a beautifully adorned contract outlining the husband's responsibilities to his wife. It is a testament to the respect and care that should define the marriage.
- **Chuppah (Wedding Canopy):** The Chuppah symbolizes the couple's new home and life together. It is usually a simple canopy under which the ceremony takes place.

Prayers and Blessings

- **Kiddushin:** This is the betrothal ceremony, where the groom presents the bride with a ring, reciting a declaration of his commitment.
- **Sheva Brachot (Seven Blessings):** These blessings celebrate the couple's love, joy, and the Divine role in their union. A glass of wine accompanies each blessing.
- **Breaking of the Glass:** One of the most iconic moments in a Jewish wedding is glass breaking. This act carries multiple interpretations. It symbolizes the fragility of life, the reminder of past sorrows, and the hope for a future filled with happiness.

A Personal Reflection

Rachel, a bride, shares her experience: *"As we stood beneath the Chuppah, surrounded by our loved ones, I felt a profound connection to my ancestors and the generations that came before us. It was a moment that transcended time, where tradition and love merged into something sacred."*

A Jewish wedding is a blend of heritage and personal expression. It reminds us that while traditions connect you to your past, love propels you into the future. It is a celebration of commitment, family, and the enduring spirit of a shared faith. In the words of the Sheva Brachot, it is a moment of *"great joy, even as the joy of creation in the Garden of Eden."*

Shiva (Mourning Practices): A Sacred Time of Reflection and Community

In the Jewish tradition, Shiva is a profound period of mourning that follows the loss of a loved one. This sad yet sacred time provides solace, support, and an opportunity for reflection on the departed's life and legacy.

Origins and Religious Significance

The roots of Shiva can be traced back to ancient Jewish customs and are deeply connected to the afterlife and the importance of community during times of grief. The word "Shiva" means seven, symbolizing the seven-day duration of this mourning period.

Observance Today

Shiva is typically observed with specific customs and rituals that offer comfort and structure to the grieving process.

Ceremonial Objects

- **Shiva Candle:** A memorial candle, called a "Yahrzeit candle," is lit at the beginning of Shiva. It burns for seven days, symbolizing the soul's eternal light.
- **Low Seating:** During Shiva, mourners often sit on low chairs or cushions, a sign of their mourning and humility.
- **Covering Mirrors:** Mirrors in the house might be covered to encourage reflection on inner qualities rather than one's physical appearance during this time.

Prayers and Readings

- **Kaddish:** The Kaddish is recited multiple times during Shiva. It praises God and expresses the hope for peace and comfort for the deceased and the mourners.
- **Psalm 23:** This psalm speaks of God as a shepherd and is a source of solace and reassurance.
- **Visiting Mourners:** Friends and family members visit the mourners to offer condolences and support. They also share stories and memories of the deceased.

A Personal Reflection

Lean, who recently observed Shiva for her father, reflects: *"During Shiva, I felt a profound sense of community and support. Friends and family came to share their condolences and stories about my dad. It was a time of grief, but also a time of remembering and celebrating his life."*

Shiva is a time-honored tradition that allows mourners to navigate the complex terrain of grief. It provides a structured space for mourning, remembrance, and community support. Through prayer, reflection, and the shared experiences of grief, Shiva reinforces the interconnectedness of life and death and the enduring bond between the living and the departed. It is a testament to the Jewish belief in the importance of memory and the power of community in times of loss.

Yahrzeit and Yizkor (Memorial Traditions): Honoring the Legacy of Loved Ones

Yahrzeit and Yizkor are significant Jewish traditions dedicated to remembering and honoring the departed. These rituals provide a structured framework for commemorating the anniversary of a loved one's passing and collectively expressing grief and remembrance.

Origins and Religious Significance

The roots of Yahrzeit and Yizkor can be traced to the Talmud and are grounded in the belief that the memory of the departed is a source of blessing and that their souls continue to influence the living. These traditions offer comfort and allow mourners to navigate the ongoing journey of grief.

Ceremonial Objects

Yahrzeit candles are lit on the anniversary of death.
Elipongo, Public domain, via Wikimedia Commons:
https://commons.wikimedia.org/wiki/File:Yahrtzeit_candle.JPG

- **Yahrzeit Candle:** A memorial candle is lit on the anniversary of the death, or Yahrzeit, and burns for 24 hours as a symbol of the soul's eternal flame.

- **Yizkor Booklets:** Prayers are recited from special booklets called Yizkor (remembrance) on Passover, Shavuot, and Yom Kippur holidays.

Prayers and Readings

- **El Malei Rachamim:** This prayer is recited at funerals and memorials and during Yahrzeit observance. It honors the memory of the departed and expresses a prayer for peace and comfort.

- **Kaddish:** The Kaddish is recited during Yahrzeit observance as a tribute to the deceased's life, deeds, and legacy.

- **Writing Notes:** Mourning families might choose to write notes or letters expressing their grief and honoring the memory of the departed on the anniversary of their passing.

A Personal Reflection

Daniel observes Yahrzeit for his mother and shares his experience: "*Lighting the Yahrzeit candle is a solemn yet comforting ritual. It's a moment when I feel close to my mother, and it's a time to reflect on the love and wisdom she shared. The Kaddish prayer reminds me that her memory is a blessing.*"

Yahrzeit and Yizkor are traditions that serve as a testament to the Jewish belief in the enduring impact of a life lived with purpose and love. Through these rituals, the living remember and continue to honor the legacy of those who have passed, finding solace in the timeless bond between generations.

Hachnasat Kallah (Bridal Shower): Celebrating Love and Unity

Hachnasat Kallah is a celebration of love and unity before a wedding. It is a joyful occasion where friends and family come together to honor the bride, shower her with blessings and gifts, and express their support for the new chapter in her life.

Origins and Religious Significance

The roots of Hachnasat Kallah can be traced back to ancient Jewish customs of hospitality and community support. It embodies the Jewish values of love, kindness, and coming together to support one another during significant life events.

Ceremonial Objects

Hachnasat Kallah is a heartfelt and festive event that precedes the wedding ceremony.

- **Kallah's Gift:** Friends and family present the bride with a gift to help her start her new life with her husband. This may include home furnishings, kitchen items, or jewelry.
- **Honey Jar:** The bride is presented with a jar of honey and coins to symbolize a sweet and fruitful life ahead.
- **Blessing Card:** Guests present the bride with a special card containing blessings for her future happiness and joy.

Prayers and Readings

- **Mi Shebeirach:** This prayer is recited to bestow blessings, peace, health, and success upon the couple as they embark on their new life together.

- **Ketubah:** The Ketubah, or marriage contract, is read in the presence of two witnesses and signed by the bride and groom. It serves as a reminder of their commitment to one another.

A Personal Reflection

Rebecca, a bride-to-be, shares her experience: *"My Hachnasat Kallah was a beautiful celebration filled with laughter and love. It was a moment when I felt the incredible support of my friends and family as I prepared to embark on this new journey. The blessings they bestowed upon me were a source of strength and encouragement."*

Hachnasat Kallah reflects the Jewish value of community and the importance of celebrating and supporting one another during significant life transitions. It is a joyful event that not only showers the bride with gifts but also showers her with love, well wishes, and the warmth of a tight-knit community. It symbolizes the idea that, in times of change and new beginnings, the love and support of family and friends are invaluable treasures.

Aufruf: Calling Up to the Torah

Aufruf is a Jewish tradition that takes place before a wedding. It involves the groom being called to the Torah during a synagogue service. This prenuptial honor is a spiritual preparation for the upcoming marriage and a moment of celebration within the community.

Origins and Religious Significance

The origins of the Aufruf tradition can be traced to a desire to bestow blessings on the soon-to-be-wed couple and invoke Divine favor for their union. It emphasizes the importance of seeking communal and spiritual support before embarking on this significant life journey.

Observance Today

Aufruf is typically observed during the Shabbat (Sabbath) service immediately preceding the wedding.

Ceremonial Objects

While Aufruf does not involve specific ceremonial objects, it is customary for the groom to wear a special white robe called a Kittel. This robe symbolizes purity and is often worn during significant events, including weddings.

Prayers and Blessings

During the Aufruf, the groom is called to the Torah for an Aliyah (the honor of reciting a blessing before and after the Torah reading). The community gathers to witness this special moment, often followed by heartfelt blessings and well wishes for the couple.

A Personal Reflection

Jacob, a groom who recently had an Aufruf, shares his experience: *"Being called up to the Torah before my wedding was a profoundly spiritual moment. It felt like a communal embrace of our upcoming union. The blessings and support from our friends and family were incredibly meaningful."*

Aufruf is a tradition emphasizing the importance of spiritual preparation and communal support as a couple embarks on their journey into marriage. It symbolizes the shared joy and blessings that surround the union of two individuals, reminding us that love and faith are not just personal but communal experiences cherished and celebrated by the wider community.

Pidyon Haben: Redemption of the Firstborn Son

Pidyon Hanen is a cherished Jewish tradition involving a firstborn son's redemption. Rooted in biblical origins, this ceremony underscores the sanctity of life and the importance of consecrating the firstborn to God.

Origins and Religious Significance

The origins of Pidyon Haben can be traced to the biblical book of Exodus. After the Exodus from Egypt, God sanctified the firstborn sons of the Israelites, sparing them during the plague of the firstborn. As a result, the firstborn sons were dedicated to God's service. However, instead of offering their firstborn, a ritual redemption ceremony was established.

Observance Today

Pidyon Haben is typically observed on the 31st day after a firstborn son's birth. It is a joyous occasion marked by rituals and blessings.

Ceremonial Objects

- **Five Silver Coins:** Five silver coins, known as "shekalim," are given to the Kohen (a descendant of Aaron, the first High Priest) to redeem the firstborn. The coins symbolize the redemption price.

- **Candles and Wine:** Candles are lit, and a cup of wine is often used during the ceremony to recite blessings.

Prayers and Blessings

The Pidyon Haben ceremony includes the recitation of prayers and blessings. The father of the firstborn son blesses God for the commandment to redeem the child and for sanctifying the firstborns.

A Personal Reflection

Anna, a mother who recently celebrated Pidyon Haben for her son, shares her experience: *"The Pidyon Haben ceremony was a reminder of the preciousness of life and our connection to tradition. It was a moment of gratitude for the health of our child and the spiritual significance of this milestone."*

Pidyon Haben is a tradition that celebrates the sanctity of life and the continuity of Jewish heritage. It reflects the importance of acknowledging the Divine role in the survival of the firstborn and the commitment to a life of purpose and service. Through this ceremony, the Jewish community continues to honor a biblical commandment while affirming the timeless bond between the generations.

Ufruf: The Bridegroom's Procession at the Wedding

Ufruf, a cherished Jewish tradition, is a joyous prelude to the wedding ceremony. It is a celebration of the groom's upcoming marriage and an opportunity for the community to offer blessings and well wishes to the couple.

Origins and Religious Significance

The roots of Ufruf can be traced to the desire to celebrate the union of a bride and groom and to invoke Divine blessings for their marriage. It emphasizes the communal support and joy surrounding a couple's journey into married life.

Observance Today

Ufruf typically takes place during the Shabbat (Sabbath) service that precedes the wedding.

Ceremonial Objects
- **Kittel:** The groom traditionally wears a Kittel, a white robe symbolizing purity and solemnity.
- **Aliyah:** During the Ufruf service, the groom is called up to the Torah for an Aliyah, an honor that involves reciting blessings before and after the Torah reading.

Prayers and Blessings

Heartfelt blessings mark the Ufruf service and well wishes for the couple's future happiness. The community gathers to support and celebrate the couple's upcoming marriage.

A Personal Reflection

Adam, a groom who recently had an Ufruf, shares his experience: "*Ufruf was a beautiful moment of community and blessing. It was a reminder that our journey into marriage was not just about us but also about the love and support of our friends and family. The Kittel I wore was a symbol of the purity of our love and the commitment we were making.*"

Ufruf is a celebration of love and the communal support surrounding a couple as they embark on their journey into marriage. It is a joyful occasion that reaffirms the Jewish values of community, blessing, and the sanctity of marriage. Through Ufruf, the couple receives both the good wishes of their loved ones and the spiritual blessings of the community, setting the stage for a lifetime of love and partnership.

Birkat HaGomel: Blessing of Deliverance

Birkat HaGomel is a Jewish tradition rooted in gratitude and protection. It is a heartfelt prayer of thanksgiving offered by individuals who have emerged from situations of danger or distress, acknowledging God's deliverance and seeking Divine protection for the future.

Origins and Religious Significance

The origins of Birkat HaGomel can be traced to the biblical book of Psalms, where King David expressed gratitude for his deliverance from perilous situations. Over time, this expression of thanks evolved into a formalized prayer. Birkat HaGomel underscores the Jewish belief in recognizing and acknowledging the blessings of safety and protection.

Observance Today

Birkat HaGomel is typically recited during synagogue services, often on Shabbat or other days when the Torah is read.

Prayers and Blessings

The central element of Birkat HaGomel is the recitation of a special blessing, expressing gratitude to God for deliverance from a perilous situation. The blessing often includes the words, *"Blessed are You, Lord our God, King of the Universe, who bestows good things upon the undeserving."*

A Personal Reflection

Abigail, who recently recited Birkat HaGomel after recovering from a severe illness, shares her experience: *"Reciting Birkat HaGomel was a deeply emotional moment for me. It was a way to express my gratitude for the recovery and the support of my community. It reminded me of the fragility of life and the importance of acknowledging the blessings of protection."*

Birkat HaGomel embodies the Jewish values of gratitude and recognizing the Divine hand in our lives. It is a prayer that acknowledges both the vulnerability of human existence and the profound blessings of safety and protection. Through this tradition, individuals express their thankfulness for emerging from danger or distress and seek ongoing Divine protection for themselves and their loved ones, underscoring the enduring belief in the power of faith and gratitude.

Throughout Jewish history and culture, many meaningful traditions have been passed down from generation to generation. From Pidyon Haben to Ufruf and Birkat HaGomel, these traditions remind you of your connection to the Divine, your commitment to others, and your appreciation for life's greatest blessings.

Chapter 3: Feast Days and Fast Days

The Jewish calendar is a marvel of both historical continuity and spiritual significance. It is punctuated by a series of Feast Days and Fast Days that follow a cyclical pattern, each with its own biblical origins and profound meaning. These observances mark the passage of time and allow Jews to connect with their heritage, express their faith, and affirm their identity.

In the heart of Jewish tradition lies sacred observances and commemorations, each bearing a unique significance in the rich mosaic of Jewish life. From the joyous festivity of Passover to the deep introspection of Tisha B'Av, each Feast Day and Fast Day carries its unique significance.

Feast Days are joyful occasions, such as Shabbat, Passover (Pesach), and Sukkot (the Feast of Tabernacles). On these days, observant Jews refrain from labor and gather in synagogue services to celebrate the bounty and blessings that God has bestowed upon them. Festive food is often involved, with unique dishes prepared and shared with family and friends.

In contrast, Fast Days are solemn religious days of mourning and reflection. These include days associated with sadness or historical tragedy. Observant Jews fast on these days and attend synagogue services to remember and reflect upon the gravity of such events.

Passover (Feast): Celebration of Tradition, Faith, and Freedom

Passover, known as Pesach in Hebrew, is one of the most cherished Jewish holidays, symbolizing the journey from bondage to freedom. It tells the story of the Israelites' liberation from slavery in Egypt and serves as a testament to the Jewish spirit's resilience and faith.

Rituals and Traditions

The Seder plate symbolizes Exodus and slavery.
Edsel Little, CC BY-SA 2.0 <https://creativecommons.org/licenses/by-sa/2.0>, via Wikimedia Commons: https://commons.wikimedia.org/wiki/File:Passover_Seder_plate,_original.jpg

- **The Seder Plate**: The Seder, held on the first two nights of Passover, revolves around the Seder plate. This plate bears symbolic foods representing the Exodus, like bitter herbs (Maror) for the bitterness of slavery and sweet charoset for the mortar used by the Israelites.

- **Matzah**: Unleavened bread, matzah, is consumed during the Seder to remember the haste of the Israelites' departure. Its simplicity signifies humility and unwavering faith.

- **Four Cups of Wine**: Represents stages of the Exodus embody God's promises, deliverance, redemption, and acceptance of the Jewish people.

Food Customs

- **Matzah Ball Soup:** A beloved Passover dish, matzah ball soup comforts with its lightness, symbolizing hope for a bright future.
- **Gefilte Fish:** Groundfish represents renewal and a new beginning, paralleling the Israelites' journey.
- **Charoset:** Apples, nuts, wine, and spices in charoset evoke the mortar used by the Israelites. It's a sweet reminder of resilience and life's sweetness.

Prayers and Symbols

Passover invites deep prayer and reflection, guided by the Haggadah. It shares the Exodus story, blessings, and songs for participants of all ages. Passover isn't just history. It's a living narrative connecting generations. Families share ancestral stories, adding a personal touch to the biblical tale. Young ones ask the Four Questions, sparking lively discussions on Passover's significance.

Passover customs vary among Jewish communities, reflecting diverse traditions. Yet, the core themes of liberation, faith, and identity preservation unite Jews worldwide. It's a holiday weaving history, faith, and family. It melds the past with the present, reminding followers of Exodus' legacy and the importance of tradition, faith, and freedom for generations. It's not merely a feast of food but a feast of the soul, celebrating hope and renewal in the human spirit.

Shavuot (Feast): Celebrating Revelation and Abundance

Shavuot, often referred to as the "Festival of Weeks," is a significant Jewish holiday that commemorates the giving of the Torah at Mount Sinai. It's a celebration of Divine revelation, spiritual renewal, and the abundance of the harvest season.

Rituals and Traditions

- **All-Night Torah Study:** Many Jewish communities engage in an all-night Torah study session known as Tikkun Leil Shavuot. It symbolizes the Jews' eagerness to receive the Torah and reflects their commitment to lifelong learning.
- **Dairy Delights:** A Shavuot tradition involves consuming dairy-based foods like cheesecakes and blintzes. This custom's origins

are varied, but it is often linked to the idea that the Torah is likened to milk and honey, signifying its sweetness and nourishment.

- **Decorating with Greenery:** Homes and synagogues are adorned with greenery and flowers to celebrate the flourishing of nature during the spring harvest. It's a visual reminder of the abundance that Shavuot represents.

Food Customs

- **Dairy Delicacies:** Cheesecakes, blintzes, and other dairy treats take center stage during Shavuot. These dishes symbolize the sweetness and richness of the Torah's teachings.
- **Fruits and Vegetables:** Fresh fruits and vegetables from the harvest season are enjoyed, connecting the holiday to the agricultural cycle in Israel.

Fresh fruits and vegetables are enjoyed during Shavuot..
https://unsplash.com/photos/Y5n8mCpvIZU?utm_content=creditShareLink&utm_medium=referral&utm_source=unsplash

Prayers and Symbols

- **Reading the Book of Ruth:** It is customary to read the Book of Ruth during Shavuot. Ruth's story of devotion and conversion reflects the commitment and inclusion themes central to the holiday.

- **The Ten Commandments:** Synagogues often conduct a special reading of the Ten Commandments on Shavuot morning, emphasizing the giving of the Torah at Mount Sinai.

Variations across Communities

Shavuot customs vary among Jewish communities, but the core celebration of receiving the Torah and the holiday's agricultural significance remain consistent. Each community infuses its unique cultural elements into the celebration, making Shavuot a vibrant and diverse festival.

Personal Narratives

Miriam, a Shavuot enthusiast, shares her experience: "*Shavuot is a time when we come together to celebrate the Torah's wisdom and the beauty of our tradition. The all-night study sessions are about learning, bonding with our community, and rekindling our spiritual connection.*"

Whether through late-night study, dairy delicacies, or the reading of Ruth's story, Shavuot invites Jews to renew their commitment to their faith and celebrate life's abundance. It's a time when the spiritual and the earthly harmonize in a joyous feast of gratitude and learning.

Tisha B'Av (Fast): Commemorating Tragedy and Seeking Redemption

Tisha B'Av, the ninth day of the Hebrew month of Av, is a solemn Jewish day of mourning and fasting. It commemorates the destruction of the First and Second Temples in Jerusalem and serves as a time for reflection on Jewish history, tragedies, and the hope for ultimate redemption.

Rituals and Traditions

- **Fasting:** One of the central observances of Tisha B'Av is fasting from sunset to the following nightfall. The fast extends to all food and drink, symbolizing a collective mourning and repentance.

- **Reading the Book of Lamentations (Eicha):** The Book of Lamentations, attributed to the prophet Jeremiah, is read on Tisha B'Av. It vividly portrays Jerusalem's destruction and the Jewish people's suffering. The haunting verses evoke deep emotions and reflections on past tragedies.

- **Sitting on the Floor:** Sitting on the floor or low stools during Tisha B'Av is customary, symbolizing mourning. Many people

also refrain from wearing leather shoes as a sign of humility.
Food Customs
Seudah HaMafseket: Before the fast begins, there is a custom to eat a simple, mournful meal called Seudah HaMafseket. It typically includes bread, a hard-boiled egg, and water or other non-alcoholic beverages.
Prayers and Reflections
Special prayers and liturgical poems called Tefillah are recited on Tisha B'Av, including the recitation of Kinot, elegies that lament the historical tragedies of the Jewish people. These prayers emphasize collective repentance and a yearning for spiritual renewal.
Symbols and Stories
Tisha B'Av is marked by a somber atmosphere, with communities coming together to remember the losses of the past. Personal stories of resilience and survival during difficult times are often shared to impart a sense of hope and continuity.

Tisha B'Av is observed with similar themes across Jewish communities worldwide, but customs and traditions may vary. Some communities focus on additional historical tragedies, while others emphasize the spiritual and personal aspects of the day.
Personal Narratives
Reflecting on Tisha B'Av, David shares his thoughts: "*Tisha B'Av is a day when we collectively grieve our history's painful moments. It's a reminder of the resilience of the Jewish people and our unwavering hope for a brighter future.*"

Tisha B'Av is a day of profound reflection, mourning, and hope. It connects Jews across the globe to their shared history and the enduring spirit of their people. The fast serves as a reminder of past tragedies, while the prayers and stories inspire a sense of unity and the collective hope for a better future. Tisha B'Av is a testament to the Jewish people's ability to remember, endure, and ultimately seek redemption.

Purim (Feast): Celebrating Survival with Joy and Unity

Purim, the festive Jewish holiday, is a joyous occasion that celebrates the survival of the Jewish people in ancient Persia. It's a time of revelry, unity, and reflection on the resilience of the Jewish spirit. Purim is marked by unique rituals, delectable food customs, heartfelt prayers, and symbols that tell a remarkable tale of triumph.

Rituals and Traditions
- **Reading the Book of Esther (Megillah):** Purim's centerpiece is reading the Book of Esther or the Megillah. This biblical tale tells of Queen Esther, who, with the help of her uncle Mordecai, courageously thwarted the wicked Haman's plot to annihilate the Jews. As the Megillah is read aloud, participants use noisemakers called "graggers" to drown out Haman's name whenever it is mentioned, adding a playful and communal aspect to the reading.

- **Costumes (Masquerade):** Purim is a time of masquerade and costume parties. Participants dress up as characters from the Purim story, animals, or even pop culture icons. The tradition of wearing costumes is a reminder that sometimes salvation comes from unexpected sources, just as Esther's identity was initially concealed.

Participants dress up as characters from the Purim story.
Arthur Szyk, Public domain, via Wikimedia Commons:
https://commons.wikimedia.org/wiki/File:Purim_by_Arthur_Szyk.jpg

- **Mishloach Manot:** On Purim, Jews exchange Mishloach Manot gift baskets filled with sweets and treats to foster community and unity. This custom underscores the importance of caring for one another and spreading joy.

Food Customs
- **Hamentashen:** Hamentashen is a beloved Purim treat, a triangular pastry filled with sweet fillings like fruit preserves or chocolate. The pastry's three corners are said to represent Haman's three-cornered hat.
- **Seudah:** A festive meal called the Seudah is enjoyed on Purim day. It typically includes traditional Jewish dishes—participants raise their glasses to celebrate their deliverance.

Prayers and Reflections

During Purim prayers, the "Al Hanissim" (For the Miracles) prayer is recited, thanking God for the miraculous events of Purim. Purim is a time when communities come together to share the story of Esther and Mordecai.

Purim is a holiday that combines revelry with reverence. It celebrates the remarkable survival of the Jewish people, the courage of Esther and Mordecai, and the enduring values of unity and caring for one another. Purim's rituals and symbols remind us of the resilience of the Jewish spirit and the importance of finding joy in the face of adversity. It's a time when the past and present merge in a delightful feast of celebration, costumes, and heartfelt gratitude.

Yom Kippur (Fast): A Day of Atonement and Spiritual Renewal

Yom Kippur, also known as the Day of Atonement, is the holiest day in the Jewish calendar. It is a solemn and reflective day marked by fasting, prayer, and repentance. Yom Kippur provides a profound opportunity for Jews to seek forgiveness, reflect on their actions, and strive for spiritual renewal.

Rituals and Traditions
- **Fasting:** The central observance of Yom Kippur is a twenty-five-hour fast, beginning at sunset and ending after nightfall the following day. This abstention from food and drink symbolizes purifying the body and soul.
- **Prayer and Synagogue Services:** Yom Kippur features an extensive series of prayers and synagogue services, including the Kol Nidre prayer recited at the start of the holiday. The day's liturgy focuses on repentance, forgiveness, and seeking God's

mercy.

- **Confession (Vidui):** Throughout Yom Kippur, Jews engage in a deep soul-searching process, acknowledging their sins and seeking forgiveness from God. The communal recitation of the Vidui prayer underscores the collective responsibility for one another's actions.

Food Customs

- **Pre-Fast Meal (Seudah HaMafseket):** Before the fast begins, there is a custom to partake in a simple meal known as Seudah HaMafseket. It typically consists of bread, a hard-boiled egg, and water or other non-alcoholic beverages.

- **Breaking the Fast (Break-Fast):** Yom Kippur concludes with a festive meal known as the break-fast. This meal includes traditional Jewish dishes and is an occasion for family and community gatherings.

Prayers and Reflections

The Neilah service is a poignant and pivotal part of Yom Kippur, emphasizing the closing of the gates of Heaven. It is a time when fervent prayers and reflections occur, and the shofar is blown to signal the conclusion of the day.

Yom Kippur is a day when communities come together to support one another in the quest for forgiveness and spiritual renewal. Personal stories of transformation and commitment to change are often shared, fostering a sense of unity and accountability.

Yom Kippur offers a unique opportunity for Jews to seek forgiveness from God and one another. It is a day when the past is acknowledged, the future is embraced, and the spirit is rejuvenated to pursue a better, more righteous life.

Asara B'Tevet (Fast): Commemorating the Siege of Jerusalem

Asara B'Tevet, the tenth day of the Hebrew month of Tevet, is a minor fast day in the Jewish calendar. It commemorates the beginning of the siege of Jerusalem by the Babylonians, a tragic event that eventually led to the destruction of the First Temple. While less known than some other Jewish fast days, Asara B'Tevet carries deep historical significance and serves as a time for reflection on the challenges faced by the Jewish people throughout history.

Rituals and Traditions

- **Fasting:** On Asara B'Tevet, Jews fast from sunrise to sunset. This fast is observed to remember the suffering of those in Jerusalem during the Babylonian siege and to express empathy for their plight.
- **Reciting Special Prayers:** During synagogue services on Asara B'Tevet, special prayers are recited, including the Selichot and penitential prayers asking for forgiveness and mercy.

Food Customs

The fast of Asara B'Tevet involves abstaining from all food and drink during daylight hours. It is a way to remember the hardship endured by those who lived through the siege of Jerusalem.

Prayers and Reflections

Selichot: The Selichot prayers on Asara B'Tevet focus on themes of repentance and forgiveness. They encourage individuals to reflect on their actions and seek reconciliation with God. Asara B'Tevet is a day when Jews remember the historical suffering of their ancestors during the Babylonian siege. It is also an opportunity to reflect on the broader themes of resilience and faith in the face of adversity.

Variations across Communities

The observance of Asara B'Tevet remains consistent across Jewish communities, with fasting and prayer as central components. While customs may vary slightly, the day's core purpose is to remember the past and reaffirm the values of repentance and spiritual introspection.

Asara B'Tevet is a day of solemn remembrance and introspection. It prompts Jews to recall the hardships of their ancestors and the importance of faith and resilience in the face of adversity. While it may not be as widely observed as other fast days, it carries the weight of history and serves as a testament to the enduring spirit of the Jewish people.

Tzom Tammuz: The Prelude to Mourning

Tzom Tammuz, a day of fasting and reflection, marks the onset of a solemn three-week period in the Jewish calendar, leading to Tisha B'Av, commemorating the destruction of both the First and Second Temples in Jerusalem. This observance is deeply rooted in history, evoking both sorrow and anticipation as Jews prepare to revisit the tragic past.

Rituals and Observance

Tzom Tammuz is observed with a sunrise-to-sunset fast, reminiscent of other Jewish fast days. While not as rigorous as Yom Kippur, it is a day marked by solemnity. As the sun rises, participants come together to engage in prayer and contemplation, reflecting on the day's historical significance.

One of the most poignant customs associated with Tzom Tammuz is reading passages from the Book of Ezekiel. This prophetic text vividly describes the events leading to the destruction of the First Temple, including the breaching of the walls of Jerusalem and the departure of the Divine Presence from the Holy Temple.

Food Customs

The fast of Tzom Tammuz ends with a modest meal, often consisting of simple and easily digestible foods. Participants break their fast with a sense of gratitude for their sustenance, appreciating the nourishment as both physical and spiritual renewal.

Symbols and Personal Narratives

Tzom Tammuz serves as a poignant reminder of the fragility of human achievements and the consequences of spiritual decay. According to tradition, breaching Jerusalem's walls on this day was a harbinger of the destruction that would follow. It was a moment when the city's defenses crumbled, signaling the impending catastrophe.

Communities worldwide share stories of resilience and hope, emphasizing the importance of spiritual renewal and unity. In many ways, Tzom Tammuz represents the beginning of a collective soul-searching period leading up to Tisha B'Av, when Jews come together to mourn the loss of their spiritual and physical center, the Holy Temple.

Variations in the observance of Tzom Tammuz can be found among different Jewish communities. Some may focus more on the historical aspects of the day, while others emphasize its broader themes of introspection and spiritual renewal.

Tzom Tammuz is a crucial moment in the Jewish calendar, signaling a period of introspection and anticipation. It reminds participators that history, even in its darkest moments, can provide valuable lessons for the present and inspire a collective commitment to spiritually and physically rebuilding. In the shadows of Tzom Tammuz lies the enduring hope for a future where unity and reverence for the Divine can prevail.

Tzom Gedaliah: Remembering with a Somber Heart

Tzom Gedaliah, a lesser-known fast day in the Jewish calendar, is a poignant reminder of the tumultuous period following the destruction of the First Temple in Jerusalem. This solemn day, which typically falls in the early days of Tishrei (the same month as Rosh Hashanah and Yom Kippur), serves as a tribute to Gedaliah ben Ahikam, a leader whose life was tragically cut short.

Rituals and Observance

Unlike the major fasts like Yom Kippur, Tzom Gedaliah is observed from dawn until nightfall, making it a relatively short fast. While the fast is not as stringent as others, its historical and spiritual significance resonates deeply with those who observe it.

The day begins with a pre-dawn meal, Seudah Mafseket, where participants eat a light meal before the fast begins. It is a moment of quiet reflection akin to the last meal of a condemned prisoner honoring Gedaliah's fate.

Throughout the day, Jews pray and contemplate, seeking spiritual connection and solace. The Book of Lamentations (Eicha) is often read as a somber text that mourns the destruction of the First Temple and the subsequent exile. Special prayers, known as selichot and penitential prayers, are also recited, highlighting the collective need for repentance and introspection.

Food Customs

Lentil soup is a traditional dish.
https://unsplash.com/photos/OMcrCX6wDpU?utm_content=creditShareLink&utm_medium=referral&utm_source=unsplash

The end of the fast is marked by a meal, usually consisting of simple and nourishing foods. Among the traditional dishes is lentil soup, a nod to Gedaliah's last meal before his assassination. Dates and pomegranates, symbolic of hope and renewal, also find their place on the post-fast table.

Symbols and Personal Narratives

Tzom Gedaliah is about preserving the memory of a leader whose life was cut short. Gedaliah ben Ahikam was known for his dedication to rebuilding the Jewish community after the destruction of the First Temple. His assassination by a fellow Jew, Ishmael ben Nethaniah, was devastating to those who had placed their hopes in him.

In observing Tzom Gedaliah, Jews come together to remember Gedaliah's commitment to unity and his tragic end. Communities share stories of resilience and the enduring spirit of a people who have faced countless trials throughout history.

Variations in observance can be found among different Jewish communities worldwide. Some may focus more on the historical aspects of the day, while others emphasize its broader themes of repentance and unity.

Tzom Gedaliah serves as a poignant reminder that Jewish history is filled with triumphs and tragedies. It encourages individuals to reflect not only on the past but also on the present and future, fostering a sense of collective responsibility and a commitment to rebuilding, even in the face of adversity.

Taanit Esther: Fasting in the Shadows of Redemption

Taanit Esther, a fast day observed on the eve of Purim, holds a unique place in the Jewish calendar. A day of somber reflection precedes the exuberant celebration of Purim. This fast day commemorates an act of great courage by Queen Esther, one that played a pivotal role in the salvation of the Jewish people.

Rituals and Observance

Taanit Esther is a dawn-to-dusk fast, akin to the observance of Yom Kippur and other significant fasts in the Jewish tradition. On this day, Jews refrain from eating and drinking, devoting themselves to prayer, introspection, and study.

One of the distinctive customs associated with Taanit Esther is the public reading of the Book of Esther, also known as the Megillah. This reading is a reminder of the events leading to the salvation of the Jews in ancient Persia and as a prelude to the grand celebration of Purim.

Food Customs

As the day of fasting draws to a close, a special meal is prepared for the evening. It is customary to break the fast with a festive feast, which includes a variety of traditional foods associated with Purim. Among these delicacies are hamantaschen, triangular pastries filled with sweet fillings, symbolizing the hidden nature of events in the Book of Esther.

Hamantaschen is usually eaten during Taanit Esther.
Eden Aviv, CC0, via Wikimedia Commons:
https://commons.wikimedia.org/wiki/File:Hamantaschen_strawberry.jpg

Symbols and Personal Narratives

Taanit Esther resonates deeply with the Jewish community because it represents the courage of Queen Esther, who, despite her fears, fasted for three days before approaching King Ahasuerus to intercede on behalf of her people. Her selflessness and bravery led to the salvation of the Jewish population in ancient Persia from the wicked Haman's plot to annihilate them.

Variations in the observance of Taanit Esther exist among different Jewish communities, with some emphasizing the historical aspects of the day and others focusing on its broader themes of courage and self-sacrifice.

Like many Jewish observances, Taanit Esther bridges the gap between historical events and contemporary relevance. It encourages individuals to draw inspiration from the past and apply it to their lives today, reminding us that even in the darkest times, the pursuit of justice and righteousness can lead to redemption and joy.

Taanit Bechorot: A Fast of Remembrance and Gratitude

Taanit Bechorot, a lesser-known fast day in the Jewish calendar, carries a profound connection to the story of the Exodus from Egypt. Observed by firstborn Jewish males on the day before Passover, it serves as a poignant reminder of the miraculous events that unfolded during that pivotal moment in Jewish history.

Rituals and Observance

Taanit Bechorot is not a full day fast like Yom Kippur or Tisha B'Av. Instead, it is a fast that spans the daylight hours, observed from sunrise until the festive Passover Seder begins in the evening. This partial fast is a way for firstborns to commemorate the special role they played in the Exodus story.

The fast begins with a morning prayer service, during which firstborns engage in introspection and gratitude for their survival. Many synagogues also offer a Siyum, a special celebration marking the completion of a tractate of the Talmud, which allows those present to break their fast.

Food Customs

One of the unique customs associated with Taanit Bechorot is the opportunity for firstborns to attend a Siyum and partake in a celebratory meal. Completing a section of the Talmud represents the joy of learning and the interconnectedness of Jewish traditions.

This celebratory meal, often held in the synagogue or a communal setting, allows firstborns to fulfill their fast day obligation and enjoy a festive reprieve before the Passover Seder.

Symbols and Personal Narratives

Taanit Bechorot is a day that draws a direct link between contemporary Jewish life and the events of the Exodus. It serves as a vivid reminder of the final plague in Egypt when the firstborn of the Egyptians perished, while the firstborn infants of the Israelites were spared, thanks to the blood of the Passover lamb on their doorposts.

While the historical events of the Exodus might seem distant, Taanit Bechorot allows firstborns to connect with the gratitude their ancestors must have felt. It is a day to reflect on the miracle of survival and the enduring legacy of the Jewish people.

Variations in the observance of Taanit Bechorot exist among different Jewish communities, with some placing greater emphasis on the historical aspects of the day and others focusing on its broader themes of gratitude and continuity.

In observing Taanit Bechorot, Jewish communities come together to reflect on the interconnectedness of their faith, heritage, and shared journey through history. It is a day that bridges the past and the present, reminding firstborns of their unique role in the Exodus story and the collective memory of the Jewish people.

In Jewish tradition, Feast Days and Fast Days offer a powerful reminder of the power of communal memory and the importance of reflection. They serve as meaningful reminders of shared heritage, collective courage, and gratitude in the face of adversity. They help you draw strength from their struggles so that you can continue to thrive even in difficult times. Through their observance, you connect with your past and find inspiration for your future.

Chapter 4: The Power of Prayer

Prayer transcends the boundaries of mere tradition, becoming a profound expression of faith. It's a sacred conduit through which individuals channel their hopes, aspirations, and gratitude to the heavens. It serves as a lifeline, binding the mortal to the immortal. It allows the human spirit to ascend and touch the Divine realm.

Prayer is an exultant song of thanksgiving in moments of celebration and joy. It's a chorus of voices raised in harmony to express gratitude for life's blessings. It becomes a wellspring of strength during adversity, offering solace and guidance when the path ahead seems obscured.

Yet, perhaps most profoundly, prayer is a powerful means of connection. It's a lifeline that links generations, a vessel through which the wisdom and devotion of the ancestors flow into the hearts of their descendants. It is a communal act, drawing individuals together in unity and shared purpose, transcending the boundaries of time and space.

Purpose of Jewish Prayer

Prayer is a direct line of communication between individuals and God.
TuBellaquito, CC BY-SA 4.0 <https://creativecommons.org/licenses/by-sa/4.0>, via Wikimedia Commons: https://commons.wikimedia.org/wiki/File:Puerto_Rican_Jew_praying.jpg

At its core, Jewish prayer is a direct line of communication between individuals and God. It serves several crucial purposes:

- **Spiritual Connection:** Prayer is a means for Jews to establish and nurture a personal relationship with God. Through prayer, they express their faith, devotion, and desire for spiritual connection.

- **Guidance and Reflection:** Jewish prayer often includes reciting sacred texts and passages from the Torah, guiding ethical and moral conduct. It serves as a reminder of the principles and values that should shape one's life.

- **Gratitude and Supplication:** Prayers are offered as expressions of gratitude for the blessings received and petitions for Divine assistance, guidance, and protection during challenging times.

Role in Everyday Life

Jewish prayer is not confined to specific occasions or places of worship. Instead, it permeates daily life. The Jewish tradition encourages individuals to pray regularly, with prescribed prayers for morning, afternoon, and evening. This consistent practice fosters mindfulness of the Divine in daily activities.

- **Morning Blessings**: Upon awakening, Jews offer blessings that express gratitude for the gift of life and the renewal of each day. This morning ritual, known as "Birkot Hashachar," sets a positive tone for the day ahead.
- **Amidah:** The "Amidah," also known as the "Shemoneh Esrei," is a central prayer recited multiple times daily. It consists of eighteen or nineteen blessings, depending on the time and day. It encompasses many themes, from praise and gratitude to requests for healing and redemption.
- **Sabbath and Festivals:** On the Sabbath and Jewish holidays, special prayers and blessings are recited to mark and celebrate these sacred times, enhancing their significance.

Structure of Traditional Jewish Prayer

Traditional Jewish prayer follows a structured format that has evolved over centuries. It is primarily conducted in Hebrew, the sacred language of Judaism, but translations are often available for those who may not be fluent in it.

- **Kavanah (Intention):** Before prayer begins, it is essential to have the proper intention and focus. This involves preparing one's heart and mind to connect sincerely with God.
- **Shema:** The recitation of the "Shema" is a pivotal moment in Jewish prayer, declaring the oneness of God. The "V'ahavta" often follows it, emphasizing the commandment to love God.
- **Amidah:** The Amidah is a cornerstone of Jewish prayer. It consists of specific blessings and sections, each with a distinct theme, such as praise, requests for forgiveness, and petitions for health and peace.
- **Reading and Torah Study:** Many prayer services include reading passages from the Torah and other sacred texts, providing an

opportunity for study and reflection.

- **Concluding Blessings:** Prayers typically conclude with gratitude and hope, reinforcing the connection between the individual and the Divine.

Jewish prayer is a multifaceted practice that shapes the spiritual lives of Jewish individuals. Its purpose extends beyond mere ritual, encompassing connection, reflection, and gratitude. The structured format of traditional Jewish prayer ensures that this rich tradition continues to thrive and remains a central part of Jewish identity and devotion.

Shema: Declaration of Faith

The Shema, perhaps the most iconic prayer in Judaism, originates from the Torah, specifically the Book of Deuteronomy (6:4-9). It is a cornerstone of Jewish prayer and belief, encapsulating the central monotheistic tenet of Judaism: the belief in one God. Traditionally, the Shema is recited twice daily, both in the morning and evening, as a way for Jews to affirm their faith and devotion.

Time and Context

The recitation of the Shema is deeply woven into the daily lives of observant Jews. In the morning, it's an integral part of the Shacharit (morning) prayer service; in the evening, it's included in the Maariv (evening) prayer service. Reciting the Shema is a ritual performed at home, often before bedtime, creating a sacred connection between individuals, their faith, and their families.

Spiritual and Cultural Significance

The Shema is a powerful declaration of Jewish faith and identity. Its words, "Hear, O Israel, the Lord our God, the Lord is One," encapsulate the essence of monotheism and the unique relationship between God and the Jewish people.

Personal and Communal Aspects

The Shema is a daily reminder of the Jewish commitment to God. It's a prayer of unity, both in its message of the oneness of God and in its practice. Families gather to recite it together, strengthening their bonds and passing their faith on to the next generation.

Jacob Shares His Experience: *"Reciting the Shema with my children before bedtime is a sacred family ritual. It brings us closer to our faith and each other. It's a moment of tranquility, reflection, and love."*

The Shema is a deeply personal and communal experience. The rhythmic cadence of its words, the emotional resonance of its message, and the bonds it forges within families and communities make the Shema a prayer that truly comes to life in the hearts and minds of those who recite it.

Amidah: Standing Prayer

The Amidah, often called the "Standing Prayer," is one of the most essential and central prayers in Jewish liturgy. Its origins can be traced back to the Second Temple period, and its composition is attributed to the Great Assembly (Anshei Knesset HaGedolah). This prayer represents a spiritual journey, guiding individuals from praise and gratitude to personal supplication.

Time and Context

The Amidah is recited multiple times daily, forming the core of the three daily prayer services: Shacharit (morning), Mincha (afternoon), and Maariv (evening). It's a momentous part of synagogue services, and its recitation in a minyan (a quorum of ten Jewish adults) holds special significance. Beyond the synagogue, it is also recited privately, allowing individuals to engage in personal and intimate conversations with the Divine.

Spiritual and Cultural Significance

The Amidah is a spiritual voyage that encapsulates the spectrum of human experience. It begins with praise for God's majesty, moves into gratitude for His providence, and culminates in personal requests. This structured progression allows Jews to connect deeply and personally with God while acknowledging their place within the broader Jewish community.

Personal and Communal Aspects

In synagogue settings, the Amidah is often recited while standing, reflecting the Jewish tradition of approaching God with reverence and respect. While the words of the prayer remain consistent, the personal supplications inserted into the "Shema Koleinu" (Hear Our Voice) section allow individuals to express their unique needs and concerns.

David Shares His Experience: *"During the Amidah, I feel a profound connection to my faith and my community. When I recite my supplications, it's as if I'm pouring my heart out to God, and I know I'm not alone in my hopes and struggles."*

The Amidah is a transformative experience that brings individuals closer to God and their fellow worshippers. Its rhythmic flow, progression from praise to personal petition, and ability to foster a sense of belonging within the Jewish community make the Amidah a dynamic and deeply cherished prayer. It is a moment of spiritual elevation that transcends the boundaries of time and place, uniting Jews in a shared faith journey.

Kaddish: Prayer for the Dead

The Kaddish is a powerful and deeply symbolic Jewish prayer for the dead. Its origins can be traced back to the Mishnah, a foundational Jewish text dating to the second century CE. Over the centuries, the Kaddish has become a central element of Jewish mourning and remembrance rituals.

Time and Context

The Kaddish is recited during specific moments in the Jewish mourning process. It is commonly recited during the mourning period (Shiva) that follows the death of a loved one. Additionally, it is a prominent feature of the Yizkor service, which takes place on Yom Kippur and other major Jewish holidays. The Yizkor service allows one to remember and pray for deceased family members and friends.

Spiritual and Cultural Significance

The Kaddish holds profound spiritual significance for Jews. It is a testament to the enduring bond between the living and the departed souls. While it is a prayer for the dead, it does not mention death. Instead, it praises and sanctifies God's name, affirming that God is compassionate, even in the face of loss and grief.

Personal and Communal Aspects

Reciting the Kaddish is a communal practice that brings together mourners and the congregation. It is often said in a minyan, a quorum of ten Jewish adults, underscoring the importance of community support during times of mourning.

The Kaddish is a prayer of connection and remembrance. Its rhythmic and repetitive cadence provides a comforting structure for mourners to express their grief and honor the memory of their loved ones. It is a reminder that, even in times of sorrow, the Jewish community stands together to support one another and reaffirm their faith in God's compassion and justice.

Birkat HaMazon: Grace after Meals

Birkat HaMazon, commonly known as the Grace after Meals, is a Jewish prayer of gratitude recited after eating a meal that includes bread. Its origins can be traced to biblical times when it was established as an expression of thanksgiving for the sustenance provided by God.

Time and Context

This prayer is traditionally recited after consuming a meal that includes bread. It is an integral part of Jewish dining etiquette, emphasizing the importance of acknowledging God's role in providing nourishment. Whether at a festive Shabbat dinner, a Passover Seder, or a simple weekday lunch, Birkat HaMazon reminds Jews of the sacred connection between physical sustenance and spiritual gratitude.

Spiritual and Cultural Significance

Birkat HaMazon is a powerful reminder of the Jewish value of gratitude. It transforms a mundane act like eating into a spiritual experience, fostering mindfulness and appreciation for the blessings of sustenance. The prayer acknowledges God's role as the ultimate provider and expresses gratitude for abundant nourishment.

Personal and Communal Aspects

While Birkat HaMazon can be recited individually, it is often done in a group setting, further reinforcing the communal bonds of sharing a meal. Reciting the prayer together amplifies the sense of unity and gratitude within the community.

David Shares His Experience: *"I remember the first time I recited Birkat HaMazon with my family. It was a moment of togetherness, gratitude, and reflection on the simple yet profound act of sharing a meal."*

Birkat HaMazon transcends the mere act of saying thanks for a meal. Its rhythmic and melodic recitation adds a layer of spirituality to eating. It brings a sense of mindfulness, reminding Jews to appreciate the blessings of sustenance and the communal bonds formed around the dinner table. Birkat HaMazon is a timeless tradition that nourishes the body and the soul, uniting individuals in gratitude and reminding them of the sacredness of everyday life.

Tefillin and Tallit: Prayer Accessories

Tefillin and Tallit, often called "phylacteries" or "prayer shawls" in English, are two essential prayer accessories in Jewish tradition. Their origins can be traced back to biblical and Talmudic times, where they were established as powerful tools for connecting with God through prayer.

Tefillin

Tefillin Shel Yad (Hand Tefillin): Tefillin for the hand consists of two small black boxes containing verses from the Torah, bound to the arm with leather straps. They serve as a tangible reminder of God's commandments.

Tefillin Shel Rosh (Head Tefillin): Tefillin for the head is worn with black leather straps that rest on the forehead and encircle the head. They symbolize the connection between thoughts and actions in serving God.

Head Tefillin symbolizes the connection between thoughts and actions in serving God.
Davidbena, CC BY-SA 4.0 <https://creativecommons.org/licenses/by-sa/4.0>, via Wikimedia Commons: https://commons.wikimedia.org/wiki/File:Kesher_Dalet_on_Head_Tefillin.jpg

Tallit

The Tallit is a prayer shawl with special fringes known as tzitzit attached to its four corners. These fringes serve as a reminder of the commandments and the Jewish identity. The Tallit is typically worn during morning prayers, particularly on weekdays and Shabbat.

Time and Context

Tefillin: Jewish men traditionally don Tefillin every weekday morning during the Shacharit prayer. This practice symbolizes their commitment to fulfilling God's commandments and connecting with Him through the recitation of prayers.

Tallit: The Tallit is worn during morning prayers, primarily during the Shacharit service, but it can also be worn on other occasions, like during Torah reading and certain holiday prayers.

Spiritual and Cultural Significance

Tefillin: Tefillin is a tangible expression of Jewish devotion and obedience to God's commandments. They are a constant reminder of the covenant between God and the Jewish people, reinforcing the importance of mindfulness and adherence to His teachings.

Tallit: The Tallit envelops the worshipper, creating a sacred space for prayer. Its tzitzit fringes are a tactile reminder of God's presence and commandments, fostering a spiritual focus during prayer.

Personal and Communal Aspects

Tefillin: Putting on Tefillin is a deeply personal and intimate daily ritual. It is also a communal practice in synagogues, where men come together to pray and connect with God.

Tallit: When draped over the shoulders, the Tallit symbolizes the shared commitment to Jewish tradition and faith. It is a visible sign of a Jew's dedication to their heritage.

Tefillin and Tallit are not mere accessories but sacred garments that serve as conduits for spiritual connection. These prayer accessories testify to the enduring traditions that enrich Jewish prayer. They reinforce the bonds between individuals, their faith, and their heritage.

Kiddush Levana: Blessing of the Moon

Kiddush Levana, also known as the Blessing of the Moon, is a unique Jewish ritual that celebrates the New Moon. Its origins can be traced to ancient Jewish texts, including the Talmud, where it is mentioned as a way to offer blessings and prayers under the moonlight.

Time and Context

Kiddush Levana is typically performed on a clear, moonlit night, preferably during the first half of the Hebrew month when the moon is waxing. It is not performed during the darkest nights of the month, especially during the moon's transition from waning to waxing.

Spiritual and Cultural Significance

This ritual is rooted in the belief that the moon represents the cyclical nature of time and serves as a symbol of renewal and rebirth. By reciting blessings and prayers under the moon, Jews connect with the rhythms of nature and affirm their faith in the Creator.

Personal and Communal Aspects

Kiddush Levana is often performed in a communal setting, such as after-evening synagogue services. However, individuals can conduct it alone or with their families at home. It fosters a sense of unity among those who gather under the moon's glow, reminding them of their shared connection to Jewish tradition and the natural world.

Kiddush Levana brings Jews closer to nature's rhythms and the Divine presence. Reciting blessings and prayers under the moon's gentle light fosters a deep connection to both the Creator and the natural world. It's a ritual that transcends time and place, reminding Jews of their traditions' enduring beauty and connection to the cosmos.

Havdalah: Separation of Shabbat

Havdalah, which means "separation" in Hebrew, is a Jewish ritual that marks the end of the sacred day of Shabbat (Sabbath) and the transition back into the regular workweek. Its origins can be traced to the Talmud, where it is described as a way to distinguish between the holy and the mundane.

Time and Context

Havdalah is performed on Saturday night after the stars come out and Shabbat officially concludes. It is traditionally done at home but can also be observed in a communal setting. The ritual is meant to be performed shortly after nightfall.

Spiritual and Cultural Significance

Havdalah is a poignant moment that encapsulates the essence of Shabbat. It serves as a reminder of the sacredness of this day of rest and reflection while also preparing individuals for the challenges and opportunities of the coming week. The ritual's blessings involve all five senses, from the sight of the braided candle's flame to the sweet fragrance of spices, engaging worshippers in a multisensory experience.

Personal and Communal Aspects

Havdalah is often a family affair, with loved ones gathering to bid farewell to Shabbat and welcome the new week together. It's a time of reflection, gratitude, and hope for the week ahead. The communal aspect of Havdalah reinforces the bonds of family and community, emphasizing the importance of shared traditions.

Havdalah encourages Jews to carry the spiritual essence of Shabbat with them into the week, infusing their daily lives with mindfulness and purpose. The ceremony's poetic blessings and sensory elements make it a profound and cherished tradition that helps bridge the gap between the sacred and the everyday.

Birkat Kohanim (Priestly Blessing): Divine Benediction

The Birkat Kohanim, also known as the Priestly Blessing, is a significant Jewish blessing that traces its origins to the Torah, specifically in the Book of Numbers (6:23-27). This blessing is traditionally bestowed by the descendants of Aaron, the priests (Kohanim), upon the congregation.

Time and Context

The Birkat Kohanim is commonly recited during synagogue services, particularly during the Musaf (additional) service on Shabbat and Jewish festivals. It is an essential part of these gatherings, signifying a special connection with the Divine.

Spiritual and Cultural Significance

This blessing holds immense spiritual significance for Jews. It invokes God's protection, grace, and favor upon the congregation. The threefold repetition of the blessing is often likened to ascending levels of holiness. The repetition intensifies its potency and reaffirms the importance of invoking God's blessings in communal worship.

Personal and Communal Aspects

While the priests recite the Birkat Kohanim, it is meant for the entire congregation's benefit. Congregants extend their hands and bow their heads to receive the blessings, creating a profound sense of unity and shared spirituality. It is a moment of communal connection with God and a reminder of the priestly duties outlined in the Torah.

The Birkat Kohanim is a sacred moment of connection between the priests, the congregation, and God. Its timeless words and gestures transcend time and space, unifying Jews in their shared faith and heritage. It is a powerful affirmation of God's presence in their lives and a source of comfort and inspiration in times of worship and communal gathering.

Yizkor: Memorial Prayer

Yizkor, the Memorial Prayer, is a solemn and deeply emotional Jewish prayer that allows individuals to remember and honor their departed loved ones. Its origins can be traced to the medieval period, and it has become an integral part of Jewish mourning and remembrance rituals.

Time and Context

Yizkor is recited on four specific occasions during the Jewish year: Yom Kippur, Shemini Atzeret (the eighth day of Sukkot), the last day of Passover, and Shavuot. These moments align with major Jewish holidays, emphasizing the connection between remembering the deceased and celebrating the Jewish calendar.

Spiritual and Cultural Significance

Yizkor is a profound expression of grief, love, and remembrance. It allows individuals to connect with the memories of their departed relatives and friends, ensuring that their legacies endure. The prayer reflects the Jewish belief in the soul's eternal nature and the importance of keeping the memory of loved ones alive.

Personal and Communal Aspects

Yizkor is typically recited in a synagogue setting, where a congregation of worshippers comes together to remember their departed family members and friends collectively. It is a communal act of remembrance that underscores the importance of support and empathy during mourning.

Ariel Shares Her Experience: *"Yizkor is a deeply personal and emotional moment for me. It's a time when I can reflect on the love and wisdom my grandparents shared with me. Being in a room filled with others who are also remembering their loved ones reminds me that I'm not alone in my grief."*

Yizkor is a poignant reminder of the enduring bonds between the living and the departed. It is a sacred moment that bridges the gap between past and present, ensuring that the memories of loved ones remain vibrant and cherished. The prayer's heartfelt words and communal context offer solace, support, and a profound connection to those who have passed on.

Tashlich: Casting Away Sins

Tashlich, which means "casting off" in Hebrew, is a symbolic Jewish ritual observed during the High Holy Days, specifically on Rosh Hashanah, the Jewish New Year. Its origins can be traced back to biblical times when the Prophet Micah spoke of God casting sins into the depths of the sea (Micah 7:19). Tashlich has since evolved into a tangible expression of seeking forgiveness and spiritual renewal.

Time and Context

Tashlich is typically performed on the first day of Rosh Hashanah or the second day if the first falls on Shabbat. It is customarily conducted near a body of flowing water, such as a river, stream, or ocean. The setting adds a profound dimension to the ritual, symbolizing the cleansing and renewal of the soul.

Spiritual and Cultural Significance

This ritual embodies the Jewish concept of *teshuvah*, which means repentance or return. Tashlich provides an opportunity for self-reflection and the symbolic casting away of sins and regrets. By releasing breadcrumbs or small objects into the water, participants metaphorically let go of their transgressions, seeking forgiveness from God.

Personal and Communal Aspects

Tashlich is often performed in a communal setting, with congregations or families gathering by the water's edge. Together, they engage in prayer, reflection, and the casting off of breadcrumbs. This communal aspect enhances the sense of shared responsibility for spiritual growth and forgiveness.

Tashlich encapsulates the essence of the High Holy Days—repentance, renewal, and the hope for a better future. It is a symbolic journey of introspection and reconciliation with God and oneself. The act of casting away sins into the flowing water is a tangible representation of the desire for spiritual growth and a clean slate in the coming year. Tashlich is a timeless reminder that, despite our imperfections, the path to forgiveness and renewal is always within reach.

Prayer plays an essential role in the Jewish faith and culture. Through rituals such as Birkat Kohanim, Yizkor, and Tashlich, Jews commune with God and remember their loved ones. These powerful acts of worship connect people and the Divine. They also serve as a reminder that you are capable of renewal and growth despite your shortcomings. By consciously engaging in these rituals, Jews find spiritual comfort, strength, and connection with God.

Chapter 5: Symbols and Sacred Objects

Judaism, one of the world's oldest monotheistic religions, is rich in symbolism and sacred objects with profound spiritual and cultural significance. These symbols and objects serve as tangible expressions of faith, reminders of history, and tools for worship and observance.

Beyond their religious significance, Jewish symbols and sacred objects are cultural touchstones. They evoke a sense of heritage and shared history among Jewish communities worldwide. They are often incorporated into art, jewelry, and architecture, reflecting the enduring legacy of the Jewish people.

Jewish symbols and sacred objects are not just artifacts. They are vessels of meaning, spirituality, and cultural identity. They connect Jews to their faith, history, and one another, bridging the gap between the tangible and the Divine in Jewish life and tradition.

Bridges to the Divine

Within Jewish tradition, symbols and sacred objects hold a profound and multifaceted significance. They serve as tangible bridges that connect the physical world to the spiritual realm. These items are not mere ornaments but conduits for spiritual connection, weaving together faith, history, and culture with deep meaning.

They enable individuals to transcend the boundaries of time and space. They facilitate a profound engagement with faith, history, and culture.

These items embody the essence of Judaism itself. It's a tradition that cherishes the tangible and the intangible, the earthly and the Divine, and the past, present, and future. All these possess deep meaning that continues to inspire and connect generations of Jewish people worldwide.

Menorah: Seven-Branched Candelabrum

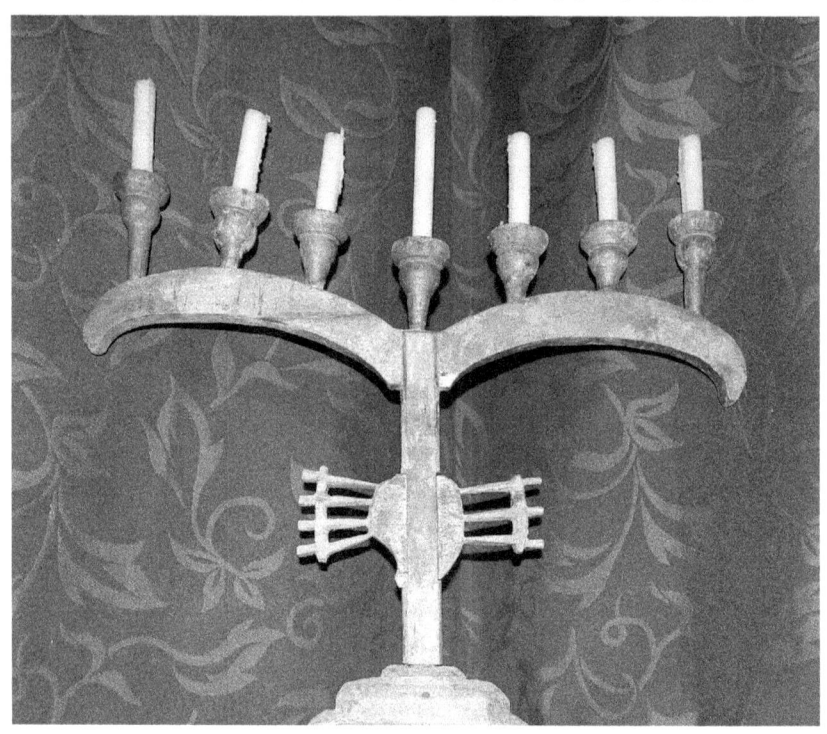

The Menorah symbolizes Jewish faith and tradition.
Jerónimo Roure Pérez, CC BY-SA 4.0 <https://creativecommons.org/licenses/by-sa/4.0>, via Wikimedia Commons:
https://commons.wikimedia.org/wiki/File:Menor%C3%A1_de_un_jud%C3%ADo_converso,_Siglo_XVI._Conservado_en_el_Palacio_de_los_Olvidados.jpg

The Menorah, a seven-branched candelabrum, is a timeless symbol of Jwish faith and tradition. With roots tracing back to biblical times, it carries deep religious and historical significance in Jewish practice.

History and Religious Significance

The Menorah's history dates back to the instructions God gave Moses in the Book of Exodus. Its seven branches represent the seven days of Creation, symbolizing God's creative power. Lighting the Menorah signifies the Divine light illuminating the world and the Jewish people's role as a light unto the nations. The construction of pure, beaten gold symbolizes spiritual refinement and holiness.

Use in Today's Practice

The Menorah remains central in contemporary Jewish life.

- **Hanukkah:** The Hanukkah Menorah, known as the Hanukkiah, commemorates the miracle of the oil that burned for eight days in the rededicated Second Temple. It is lit during the eight nights of Hanukkah, symbolizing joy and illumination.

- **Synagogue Decor:** In synagogues, the Menorah signifies God's eternal presence. A lit Menorah often graces the Ark containing the Torah scrolls.

- **Life Cycle Events:** The Menorah appears in weddings and Bar/Bat Mitzvahs, symbolizing love, commitment, and the transition to Jewish adulthood.

- **Shabbat:** Some homes display a seven-branched Menorah as a symbol of sanctity during the Sabbath.

The Menorah's enduring presence reflects its significance as a visual reminder of faith, resilience, and spiritual aspiration. It connects Jews to their heritage and Creator, providing continuity and belonging.

Star of David (Hexagram Symbol): The Emblem of Jewish Identity

The Star of David is an enduring emblem of Jewish faith and heritage.
Zscout370, Public domain, via Wikimedia Commons:
https://commons.wikimedia.org/wiki/File:Star_of_David.svg

The Star of David, the Magen David, or the Shield of David, is the quintessential symbol of Jewish identity. Its intricate design and deep-rooted history have made it an enduring emblem of Jewish faith and heritage.

History and Religious Significance

The origins of the Star of David are shrouded in history, but it became associated with Jewish identity in the late Middle Ages. Its name, Magen David, means "Shield of David," alluding to King David, the biblical hero who defeated Goliath.

Religiously, the Star of David does not have a direct scriptural reference in the Hebrew Bible. However, it has been adopted as a symbol of Divine protection and unity. The intertwining triangles symbolize the connection between God and humanity. The two triangles represent the relationship between the Divine and the earthly.

Use in Today's Practice

The Star of David holds a prominent place in contemporary Jewish life:

- **Religious Symbols:** It appears on synagogue exteriors, prayer shawls (tallit), and the covers of Torah scrolls, emphasizing its role in worship and religious practice.

- **Jewish Identity:** The Star of David is worn as jewelry, displayed on flags, and featured on gravestones, serving as a proud declaration of Jewish identity.

- **Zionism:** The symbol is associated with the Zionist movement and is featured on the flag of Israel, representing the state's Jewish character and heritage.

- **Holocaust Memorials:** The Star of David is a poignant element in Holocaust memorials, reminding the world of the tragic history of Jewish persecution.

The Star of David's enduring significance lies in its ability to encapsulate Jewish identity, faith, and history within a simple symbol. It is a reminder of the enduring strength and resilience of the Jewish people. It connects them to their past, present, and future as they contribute to human civilization.

Mezuzah: Doorpost Parchment

The Mezuzah unites daily life with Divine presence.
Deror_avi, CC BY-SA 3.0 <https://creativecommons.org/licenses/by-sa/3.0>, via Wikimedia Commons: https://commons.wikimedia.org/wiki/File:Mezuzah_IMG_2124.JPG

The Mezuzah, a small parchment inscribed with sacred verses, is a symbol of Jewish faith and tradition. Affixed to doorposts in Jewish homes, it represents a spiritual threshold, uniting daily life with Divine presence.

History and Religious Significance

The Mezuzah's origins date back to biblical times, rooted in the commandment found in the Torah: *"And you shall write [these words] upon the doorposts of your house"* (Deuteronomy 6:9). The parchment contains verses from the Shema, affirming the Jewish declaration of monotheism and love for God.

Affixing a Mezuzah is a constant reminder of God's presence and the importance of living a mindful, ethical life. The Mezuzah is more than a decorative ornament. It's a tangible expression of Jewish identity and commitment to faith.

Use in Today's Practice

The Mezuzah remains an integral part of contemporary Jewish life:

- **Home Blessing:** Affixing a Mezuzah to the doorpost is a heartfelt home blessing. As individuals pass through the doorway, they touch the Mezuzah and kiss their fingers, a gesture of reverence and connection.

- **Protection and Blessing:** The Mezuzah offers protection and blessings to those who dwell within the home. It symbolizes a commitment to living by Jewish values.
- **Community and Identity:** The presence of Mezuzot on doorposts creates a sense of community among Jewish neighbors and identifies Jewish homes. It fosters a shared faith and tradition.
- **Life Cycle Events:** Mezuzots are often gifted or placed on doorposts during life cycle events, such as weddings, new home blessings, or Bar/Bat Mitzvahs. These moments celebrate Jewish continuity and heritage.

The Mezuzah's significance extends beyond its physical presence. It represents a spiritual connection to God and a commitment to living a life of meaning and purpose. It is a daily reminder of the values and beliefs that define Jewish identity, reinforcing the sacred bond between the Divine and the everyday.

Tallit: Prayer Shawl

The Tallit, a distinctive Jewish prayer shawl, is more than a piece of clothing. It symbolizes faith, devotion, and the connection between the worshipper and the Divine. With ancient roots and deep spiritual significance, the Tallit enriches Jewish prayer and rituals.

History and Religious Significance

The history of the Tallit can be traced back to biblical times when a commandment was given in the Torah (Numbers 15:38-41) to attach fringes, known as tzitzit, to the corners of one's garments. Over time, these fringes evolved into the Tallit as it is known today.

The Tallit serves as a reminder of God's commandments and the importance of fulfilling them. The tzitzit represents the six hundred and thirteen mitzvot (commandments) found in Jewish tradition. As one dons the Tallit, it is customary to recite a blessing, emphasizing the spiritual journey and the intention to fulfill the commandments.

Use in Today's Practice

- **Prayer and Synagogue:** Jewish men wear the Tallit during daily prayer services and synagogue gatherings. It envelops them in a sacred cocoon, creating a focused environment for connecting with God.

- **Blessings and Rituals:** The Tallit is used during the recitation of the Amidah (standing prayer), a central part of Jewish worship. It is also placed over the head and shoulders during the Kol Nidre service on Yom Kippur, a poignant moment of spiritual introspection.
- **Legacy and Heirlooms:** Tallitot are often cherished family heirlooms passed down through generations, symbolizing the continuity of faith and tradition within Jewish families.

The Tallit's significance extends beyond its physical form. It envelops the worshipper in a mantle of spirituality, helping to create an atmosphere conducive to prayer and connection with God. Each wearing serves as a tangible reminder of the covenant between the Jewish people and their Creator, fostering a sense of continuity, devotion, and spiritual fulfillment.

Tefillin: Phylacteries

Tefillin, also known as phylacteries, are sacred Jewish objects symbolizing the unity of heart and mind in the service of God. These leather boxes contain verses from the Torah and are worn by Jewish men during weekday morning prayers, serving as a tangible connection to Divine commandments and a profound expression of faith.

History and Religious Significance

Wearing tefillin is deeply rooted in the Torah, specifically in the passages of Deuteronomy (6:4-9) and Exodus (13:1-10). These verses emphasize the importance of binding God's commandments "*as a sign upon your hand and between your eyes.*" Tefillin, worn on the arm and forehead, embodies this biblical directive.

Wearing tefillin signifies an individual's commitment to fulfilling God's commandments with heart and mind. The straps that bind the tefillin to the body serve as a physical connection to the Divine and a reminder of the Jewish people's unique relationship with God.

Use in Today's Practice

- **Morning Prayers:** Upon reaching the age of Bar Mitzvah, Jewish men typically wear tefillin during weekday morning prayers. This practice underscores the importance of daily connection with God and the observance of commandments.
- **Concentration and Focus:** Tefillin is a tool for heightened concentration during prayer. Binding them requires mindfulness,

ensuring that the worshipper approaches prayer with devotion and intent.

- **Spiritual Connection:** Wearing tefillin is a tangible expression of faith, symbolizing devotion to God's commandments. It is a powerful act of binding the heart and mind to serve the Divine.
- **Legacy and Tradition:** Tefillin often become cherished heirlooms passed down through generations, representing the continuity of Jewish faith and practice.

The practice of tefillin encapsulates the essence of Jewish spirituality, binding the Divine words of the Torah to one's body and soul. It is a daily ritual that reinforces the Jewish commitment to a life guided by faith, moral values, and the observance of God's commandments. Wearing tefillin is a profound act of devotion, uniting past, present, and future generations in the eternal bond between God and the Jewish people.

Torah: Scroll of the Law

The Torah is also known as the Scroll of the Law.
Kadumago, CC BY 4.0 <https://creativecommons.org/licenses/by/4.0>, via Wikimedia Commons: https://commons.wikimedia.org/wiki/File:Torah_Hebraica.png

The Torah, often called the Scroll of the Law, stands as the cornerstone of Jewish faith and identity. This sacred text, comprising the first five books of the Hebrew Bible, holds immense spiritual and historical significance for the Jewish people.

History and Religious Significance

The Torah's history is rooted in biblical accounts of the revelation at Mount Sinai, where God bestowed upon Moses the Divine commandments and teachings. These revelations were recorded in the Torah, which includes Genesis, Exodus, Leviticus, Numbers, and Deuteronomy.

The Torah contains the commandments (mitzvot) that guide Jewish ethical and moral conduct, along with the stories and narratives that shape Jewish identity. It serves as a source of wisdom, law, and spiritual guidance.

Use in Today's Practice

- **Synagogue Services:** The Torah scroll is at the heart of synagogue services, where weekly readings occur during Shabbat (the Sabbath) and on Mondays and Thursdays. The entire Torah is read over a year, starting and concluding on the holiday of Simchat Torah.

- **Bar/Bat Mitzvah:** Jewish boys and girls typically become Bar or Bat Mitzvah at thirteen. This rite of passage involves reading from the Torah during a synagogue service, signifying their responsibility to observe Jewish commandments.

- **Torah Study:** Jewish learning centers on studying the Torah and its commentaries. Torah study fosters a deep understanding of Jewish law, ethics, and values, nurturing spiritual growth and intellectual engagement.

- **Life Cycle Events:** The Torah plays a central role in life cycle events such as weddings, where it is prominently displayed, and funerals, where it signifies the importance of honoring the deceased.

The Torah is a living testament to Jewish heritage and spirituality. It guides daily life, informs moral choices, and connects generations of Jews to their shared history and faith. In its words, Jews find a code of conduct, a source of inspiration, a connection to God, and a profound affirmation of their identity as the Chosen People.

Kippah: Skullcap

The Kippah, also known as a yarmulke, is a small, circular head covering that holds profound significance in Jewish tradition. Worn by Jewish men as an expression of faith and humility, the Kippah is a visible reminder of one's connection to God and the Jewish community.

History and Religious Significance

The tradition of covering one's head as a sign of respect and reverence dates back to biblical times. In Jewish tradition, the Kippah is a reminder that God is always above and watching. It symbolizes humility, acknowledging that all are equal before the Divine.

Wearing a Kippah gained prominence in the Middle Ages, becoming integral to Jewish attire. Today, it continues to symbolize Jewish identity and faith.

Use in Today's Practice

- **Prayer and Synagogue:** Jewish men wear a Kippah during prayer services and when entering a synagogue. It signifies their respect for the sacred space and submission to God's presence.

- **Life Cycle Events:** Kippot (plural of Kippah) is often distributed at life cycle events such as Bar Mitzvahs, weddings, and other celebrations. Guests wear them as a sign of unity and participation.

- **Daily Life:** Many Jewish men wear a Kippah as part of their daily attire, signifying their constant awareness of God's presence and commitment to Jewish values.

- **Interfaith Relations:** In diverse and multicultural societies, the Kippah is a symbol of Jewish identity, fostering understanding and dialogue with people of different faiths.

The Kippah is a tangible expression of Jewish faith, humility, and commitment to God's commandments. It is a unifying symbol that transcends cultural and geographical boundaries, connecting Jews to their heritage and reinforcing their shared identity as a chosen people. Through its simple design, the Kippah reminds wearers and observers of the enduring strength of Jewish tradition and the relationship between God and the Jewish people.

Sabbath Candles: Kindling the Flame of Sacred Rest

Sabbath candles symbolize the warmth and sanctity of the Sabbath or Shabbat. As the sun sets on Friday evening, Jewish families come together to light these candles, ushering in a day of rest, reflection, and spiritual connection.

History and Religious Significance

The practice of lighting Sabbath candles has deep biblical roots. In the Book of Exodus, God commands the Jewish people to remember and observe the Sabbath day, setting it apart as holy. Lighting candles on Friday evening is a tangible expression of this sacred commandment.

Sabbath candles symbolize the physical light they emit and the spiritual illumination they bring. The flickering flames represent the Divine light, peace, and harmony at home during Shabbat. Lighting these candles is a sacred obligation, signifying the separation between the mundane and the holy.

Use in Today's Practice

- **Family Gathering:** As the sun sets on Friday evening, Jewish families gather around the table. The woman of the household, often the mother or grandmother, recites the blessing and lights the candles. The sight of the glowing candles sets a serene atmosphere.

- **Blessing and Prayer:** The lighting of the candles is accompanied by a blessing, welcoming the arrival of Shabbat. Families often recite additional prayers, expressing gratitude and invoking God's blessings upon their loved ones.

- **Peace and Tranquility:** The Sabbath candles create peace and tranquility within the home. Their gentle glow fosters a sense of serenity, fostering spiritual connection and restful contemplation.

- **Connection to Tradition:** Lighting Sabbath candles connects Jewish families to generations of Jews who have observed this tradition for millennia. It serves as a link between the past, present, and future of Jewish identity.

Sabbath candles are beacons of spirituality and reminders of the sanctity of time. They symbolize the intentional pause from the busyness of daily life to embrace the spiritual nourishment of Shabbat. As the candles burn, they illuminate the room and the hearts of those gathered, igniting a flame of unity, peace, and devotion to the eternal Jewish tradition.

Kiddush Cup: Raising the Cup of Sanctification

The Kiddush Cup is used for holding and blessing wine.
Downtowngal, CC BY-SA 4.0 <https://creativecommons.org/licenses/by-sa/4.0>, via Wikimedia Commons:
https://commons.wikimedia.org/wiki/File:Silver_kiddush_cup_given_to_Hadassah_volunteer2.jpg

The Kiddush Cup, a vessel used for holding and blessing wine, plays a central role in Jewish religious ceremonies, most notably during the Kiddush ritual on Shabbat and Jewish holidays. This elegantly designed cup symbolizes the sanctification of time, community, and the blessings of Jewish tradition.

History and Religious Significance

The tradition of sanctifying the Sabbath and festivals with wine has deep biblical roots. The Kiddush, which means "sanctification" in Hebrew, is a moment when Jews gather, often around a table, to recite blessings over wine and bread. This practice is rooted in the Torah, which commands the observance of Shabbat and the blessings that accompany it.

The Kiddush Cup is a tangible symbol of holiness. It represents not only the blessings of the wine but also the sacred nature of communal gatherings and the continuity of Jewish traditions from generation to generation.

Use in Today's Practice

- **Shabbat and Holidays:** On Friday evenings and before festive meals, Jews recite the Kiddush, holding the cup aloft and invoking blessings over the wine. This practice sanctifies the occasion and reminds participants of their covenant with God.
- **Bar/Bat Mitzvahs and Weddings:** Special Kiddush Cups are often used in life cycle events. Bar and Bat Mitzvahs, weddings, and other occasions incorporate the Kiddush Cup as a symbol of celebration and Jewish identity.
- **Community and Family:** The Kiddush Cup signifies the unity of the Jewish community and family. Passing the cup from one person to another during the Kiddush reinforces the bonds of kinship and faith.
- **Legacy and Heirlooms:** Many families possess heirloom Kiddush Cups passed down through generations. These cups serve as tangible reminders of familial and communal history.

The Kiddush Cup is a vessel for sanctification and spiritual connection. It embodies the richness of Jewish heritage, the joy of communal gatherings, and the enduring commitment to faith. As the Kiddush Cup is raised and the blessings are recited, it symbolizes the Jewish people's eternal bond with God and the enduring blessings of tradition and community.

Matzah: Unleavened Bread

Matzah is a fundamental element of Jewish tradition.
Jacek Proszyk, CC BY-SA 4.0 <https://creativecommons.org/licenses/by-sa/4.0>, via Wikimedia Commons: https://commons.wikimedia.org/wiki/File:Shmurah_Matzah_01.jpg

Matzah, the unleavened bread, is a fundamental element of Jewish tradition, particularly during the Passover holiday. This simple flatbread symbolizes the affliction of slavery and the liberation of the Jewish people.

History and Religious Significance

The history of Matzah is deeply intertwined with the biblical narrative of the exodus from Egypt. When the Israelites hastily left Egypt, they had no time for their bread dough to rise, so they baked unleavened bread, which became Matzah. It symbolizes the urgency of their departure and the willingness to embrace God's commandments.

Matzah is often referred to as the "bread of affliction." It's a powerful reminder of the hardships endured during slavery in Egypt. Its simplicity and lack of leaven represent humility and the rejection of arrogance and pride.

Use in Today's Practice

Matzah remains a central element of Jewish practice, particularly during Passover.

- **Passover Seder:** Matzah takes center stage during the Passover Seder, a special ceremony held on the first two nights of Passover. It fulfills the biblical commandment to eat unleavened bread during this holiday.

- **Symbolic Elements**: Three Matzots are traditionally placed on the Passover Seder plate, symbolizing the three stages of the Jewish people's journey: slavery, freedom, and the covenant with God.

- **Strict Dietary Observance:** Throughout the Passover holiday, Jews abstain from leavened products, eating only Matzah as a symbol of their commitment to the Passover story.

- **Remembrance and Education**: Matzah serves as a teaching tool, ensuring that future generations understand the significance of the Exodus and the importance of freedom.

Matzah is a living link to the past, a symbol of faith, and a testament to the enduring spirit of the Jewish people. It reminds Jews not only of the bitter experiences of slavery but also of the sweet taste of freedom and the responsibilities of living with compassion, humility, and a commitment to justice and righteousness.

Judaism's symbols and sacred objects have deep religious, cultural, and historical significance. They are tangible reminders of the long-standing covenant between the Jewish people and God and the commitment to freedom and justice. These symbols embody the richness of Jewish tradition, connecting Jews worldwide in one shared community committed to spiritual growth and faith. As each generation passes on its heritage, may these symbols guide you forward with compassion, humility, and hope.

Chapter 6: Musical Traditions

Music is a universal language that transcends borders and speaks to the soul. In the rich history of human culture, Jewish musical traditions stand out as a testament to the enduring connection between melody and faith. Jewish musical traditions are as diverse as the global Jewish diaspora itself. From the hauntingly beautiful chants of Sephardic Jews in Spain to the lively klezmer melodies of Eastern European Ashkenazi communities, the musical landscape reflects the multifaceted nature of Jewish identity.

Music is a universal language.
https://unsplash.com/photos/rPOmLGwai2w?utm_content=creditShareLink&utm_medium=referral&utm_source=unsplash

At the heart of Jewish music lies a profound connection to sacred texts and religious rituals. Psalms and verses from the Torah have been set to music for millennia. These create a spiritual bridge between worshipers and the Divine. Jewish music plays an integral role in religious life, whether it's the melodic recitation of prayers in the synagogue or the joyous songs of celebration during holidays.

Music's Role in Jewish Cultural Tradition

Music serves as a vehicle for spiritual expression and cultural preservation. In synagogues, cantorial music enriches the prayer experience. It guides congregants with emotional depth and intricate vocal improvisations. Wordless melodies, or Nigunim, transcend language barriers, enabling a direct connection to the Divine.

Jewish music is vital in preserving cultural heritage and transmitting customs and stories through generations. Celebrations and festivals are imbued with music. Klezmer music, known for its lively tunes, brings people together. Jewish music reflects the diversity of Jewish communities worldwide. It blends cultural elements while maintaining a distinct identity. It has also significantly contributed to the global music scene, with artists like Leonard Cohen and Bob Dylan drawing from their Jewish backgrounds.

In educational settings, music imparts Jewish values and history to young learners. It strengthens Jewish identity and cultural roots. During challenging times, music provides solace and healing. Music therapy aids emotional recovery and trauma coping within Jewish communities. Music in Jewish culture is a profound expression of faith, culture, and community. Through its various forms and styles, it preserves tradition, fosters connections, and enriches Jewish individuals' and communities' spiritual and cultural lives worldwide.

Shofar Blowing: Ancient Echoes of the Soul

The tradition of Shofar blowing is a profound and evocative form of Jewish music. The Shofar is a ram's horn, a simple yet spiritually resonant instrument. When it is sounded, its deep, haunting call reverberates with centuries of history, evoking a myriad of emotions and spiritual connections.

History and Religious Significance

The Shofar has played a significant role in Jewish tradition since biblical times. Its origins can be traced back to the story of the binding of Isaac when a ram was sacrificed in place of Abraham's son. This act of Divine intervention sanctified the ram's horn as a symbol of faith, obedience, and redemption.

The blowing of the Shofar is a key element in Jewish religious practice, particularly during the High Holidays of Rosh Hashanah (Jewish New Year) and Yom Kippur (Day of Atonement). Its distinctive sound is a wake-up call to introspection and repentance, a reminder of the need to mend one's ways and seek forgiveness.

Musical Expression

The Shofar's melodies are not complex in the way that classical compositions are, but they are rich in symbolism and emotional depth. The blasts of the Shofar can be classified into three main types:

1. **Tekiah (a Long, Solid Note)**: The Tekiah represents a call to attention, a summons to self-reflection and accountability. Its unwavering sound carries a sense of determination.
2. **Shevarim (a Broken, Trembling Note):** Shevarim, characterized by three short blasts, reflects the notion of brokenness and the need for healing. It conveys the pain of past mistakes and the hope for renewal.
3. **Teruah (a Rapid Series of Staccato Notes):** Teruah, a rapid series of nine short blasts, serves as an alarm, a cry for spiritual awakening. It carries a sense of urgency and a call to action.

The emotional impact of Shofar blowing is undeniable. It stirs the soul, resonating with feelings of a deep connection to the Divine. The sound of the Shofar is raw and primal. It transcends words and touches the innermost chambers of the heart.

Throughout history, the Shofar has played a significant role in moments of triumph and adversity. From the biblical story of Jericho's walls crumbling to the stirring accounts of Shofar blowing during the darkest days of the Holocaust, the Shofar has been a symbol of hope, resilience, and faith.

Hazzanut: Cantorial Music

Hazzanut, or cantorial music, is a profound tradition within Jewish liturgical music, weaving intricate melodies, vocal techniques, and occasionally instruments into the fabric of prayer. It is a conduit for spiritual elevation and connection to the Divine.

Melodies and Musical Elements

Hazzanut is characterized by its unique melodies and nusach, or musical modes. These modes, rooted in ancient traditions, correspond to specific times in the Jewish calendar or themes in prayers. Cantors, known as hazzanim, skillfully navigate these modes, infusing prayers with emotional depth. Though primarily vocal, Hazzanut may incorporate instruments like the violin, organ, or keyboard, enhancing the musical experience in some traditions.

Vocal Techniques

- **Cantorial Voice:** Hazzanim possesses powerful and passionate voices, using a wide range to express the liturgical text's depth.
- **Ornamentation:** Vocal ornamentation techniques, including trills and melismatic passages, enhance the singing's beauty and emotional resonance.
- **Hazzan's Krechtz:** The "hazzan's krechtz" is a guttural, emotive sound used during poignant moments, conveying longing, sorrow, or spiritual connection.

Hazzanut transcends music. It is a spiritual journey. Cantors guide congregations in prayer, leading them to connect with the Divine. Hazzanut's melodies and vocal techniques evoke emotions and foster profound spirituality within the Jewish worship experience.

Pizmonim: Sephardic Musical Treasures

Pizmonim, a vibrant tradition of Sephardic Jewish music, is a captivating combination of melodies and lyrics passed down through generations. These traditional songs are an integral part of Sephardic culture. They enrich celebrations and connect communities to their heritage.

Melodies and Musical Elements

Pizmonim encompasses many melodies and musical styles, reflecting the diverse Sephardic diaspora.

- **Ladino Lyrics:** Many Pizmonim are sung in Ladino, a Judeo-Spanish language that has preserved the linguistic and cultural heritage of Sephardic Jews.
- **Eastern and Western Influences**: The melodies blend influences from the regions where Sephardic Jews settled, incorporating elements from Spain, the Middle East, North Africa, and the Balkans.

- **Instruments**: While Pizmonim is often sung a cappella, traditional instruments like the oud, violin, and darbuka may accompany the songs, enhancing their musical depth.

Religious and Cultural Significance

Pizmonim serves various purposes in Sephardic Jewish life:

- **Liturgy:** Some Pizmonim are incorporated into religious services, enriching the worship experience with soul-stirring melodies.

- **Lifecycle Events:** These songs accompany significant life events such as weddings, circumcisions, and bar/bat mitzvahs, infusing these occasions with cultural and religious significance.

- **Holidays and Festivals:** Pizmonim are an integral part of holiday celebrations, bringing joy and a sense of community to festive gatherings.

- **Preservation of Heritage**: These songs are a living testament to the Sephardic Jewish heritage, preserving the Ladino language, cultural customs, and musical traditions.

Pizmonim bridges generational gaps, uniting young and old through the shared experience of singing these cherished songs. Whether singing in a synagogue, around a family table, or at community events, Pizmonim is a celebration of Sephardic culture and a testament to the enduring power of music to evoke emotions, preserve traditions, and strengthen communal bonds.

Klezmer: The Soulful Soundtrack of Ashkenazi Jewish Life

Klezmer, the traditional music of Ashkenazi Jews, is a spirited and evocative musical genre that embodies the rich culture of Eastern European Jewish communities. Rooted in the folk traditions of Eastern Europe, Klezmer has evolved over centuries, becoming a vibrant and cherished expression of Jewish identity.

Melodies and Musical Elements

A Klezmer band typically includes instruments such as the clarinet, violin, and trumpet.
Menachem Kipnis, Public domain, via Wikimedia Commons:
https://commons.wikimedia.org/wiki/File:KLEZPO.png

Klezmer's music is characterized by its distinctive melodies, spirited rhythms, and a fusion of musical styles from Eastern Europe, the Middle East, and the Balkans. Key elements include:

- **Instrumentation:** Klezmer bands typically include instruments such as the clarinet, violin, accordion, trumpet, and the tsimbl (a type of hammered dulcimer).
- **Ornamentation:** Musicians use ornamentation techniques like trills, glissandos, and vibratos to add expressiveness and virtuosity to their performances.
- **Modal Scales:** Klezmer melodies often employ modal scales, which give the music its distinctive Eastern European flavor.
- **Improvisation:** Improvisation is a hallmark of Klezmer music, allowing musicians to add their personal touch and creativity to traditional tunes.

Cultural and Celebratory Significance

- **Weddings:** Klezmer bands play a central role in Jewish weddings, infusing the festivities with vitality and joy. The traditional "Hora" dance, often accompanied by Klezmer music, highlights the celebration.
- **Simchas:** These joyous occasions, including bar/bat mitzvahs and circumcisions, are enhanced by the spirited melodies of Klezmer music.
- **Festivals:** Klezmer is an integral part of Jewish festivals, especially Hanukkah and Purim; its lively tunes accompany communal celebrations.
- **Yiddish Theater:** Klezmer music has also played a role in Yiddish theater, providing the musical backdrop for plays and performances.

Klezmer's music celebrates Jewish life and serves as a bridge between generations. It connects contemporary Jews with their Ashkenazi heritage. Its melodies are a testament to the resilience, joy, and cultural richness of Ashkenazi Jewish communities. It carries the spirit of a vibrant culture across time and place.

Zemirot: Harmonious Shabbat Melodies

Zemirot, the enchanting songs of the Jewish Sabbath, enriches the Shabbat experience with joy, reflection, and communal unity. These songs, sung during the Friday night and Saturday afternoon meals, infuse the Sabbath with a sense of celebration and spirituality.

Melodies and Musical Elements

Zemirot encompasses a diverse range of melodies and poetic lyrics, reflecting the beauty and tranquility of the Shabbat day.

- **Traditional Tunes:** Zemirot melodies often draw from traditional Jewish melodies, passed down through generations, and rooted in various Jewish communities worldwide.
- **Harmony and Choral Singing:** Zemirot is typically sung harmoniously, with family members and guests joining in communal singing. The harmonious voices create an atmosphere of unity and togetherness.

- **Sabbath Themes:** The lyrics of Zemirot focus on the themes of rest, gratitude, and spiritual connection, capturing the essence of the Shabbat experience.
- **Variety:** There is a wide variety of Zemirot, with some tailored explicitly for Friday night and others for Saturday afternoon, adding depth and richness to the Sabbath celebration.

Cultural and Spiritual Significance

- **Spiritual Connection:** These songs help congregants connect on a deeper level with the spiritual significance of Shabbat, creating a sense of sanctity and tranquility.
- **Family and Community Bonding:** Zemirot often involves participation from everyone present, fostering a strong sense of family and community bonding.
- **Cultural Heritage:** These melodies carry the cultural heritage of Jewish communities worldwide, preserving their unique musical traditions.
- **Expressing Gratitude:** Many Zemirot express gratitude for the blessings of Shabbat and the opportunity for rest and reflection.

Zemirot encapsulates the essence of the Sabbath, a day of rest, reflection, and renewal. These harmonious melodies evoke a sense of joy and spirituality, enhancing the Shabbat experience and creating cherished memories for families and communities worldwide.

Nigunim: The Mystical Heartbeat of Jewish Music

Nigunim, the soulful and wordless melodies of Jewish tradition, is an enchanting musical phenomenon that transcends language and speaks directly to the heart and soul. These melodies are deeply rooted in Jewish spirituality, offering a profound connection to the Divine.

Melodies and Musical Elements

Nigunim is characterized by simplicity and emotional depth, often featuring repetitive motifs that create a meditative and trance-like quality.

- **Wordlessness:** Nigunim is typically devoid of lyrics, relying solely on the power of melody to convey emotion and spirituality.
- **Repetition:** Many Nigunim are built on repetitive phrases, allowing for a deep immersion into the music and an opportunity

for contemplation.
- **Improvisation:** Nigunim provides space for improvisation, allowing musicians and congregants to infuse their spiritual experiences into the melody.
- **Harmony:** When sung in groups, Nigunim harmonizes voices, creating a communal and spiritually resonant atmosphere.

Spiritual and Communal Significance
- **Prayer and Meditation:** The melodies are often used during prayer and meditation to elevate the worshipper's spiritual experience, fostering a sense of closeness to the Divine.
- **Communal Bonding:** Nigunim is frequently sung in groups, enhancing community and unity among participants.
- **Joy and Celebration**: Nigunim can be celebratory, infusing joy and exuberance into Jewish festivities, including weddings, circumcisions, and other life events.
- **Personal Expression:** For individuals, Nigunim provides a means of personal expression and a conduit for connecting with their inner spirituality.

Nigunim is a testament to the power of music to convey emotions, express spirituality, and connect people on a profound level. They are a tradition that inspires and uplifts Jewish communities worldwide, serving as a universal language of the heart and soul.

Yemenite Jewish Music: A Timeless Tradition

Yemenite Jewish music is a unique and ancient musical tradition that reflects the rich cultural heritage of Yemenite Jews, one of the oldest Jewish communities in the world. This music carries the history, spirituality, and resilience of a people who have maintained their distinct identity for millennia.

Melodies and Musical Elements

Yemenite Jewish music is characterized by its distinctive melodies, rhythmic patterns, and cultural influences, including:
- **Traditional Yemenite Tunes:** The melodies draw from the unique scales and musical modes of Yemenite culture, creating a sound distinct from other Jewish musical traditions.

- **Vocal Harmonies:** Yemenite songs often feature intricate vocal harmonies, with singers using complex interplay to create a multi-layered and mesmerizing sound.
- **Instruments:** Traditional Yemenite instruments such as the Qanbus (a stringed instrument), drums, and hand percussion instruments contribute to the music's unique texture.
- **Liturgical and Cultural Integration:** Yemenite Jewish music seamlessly blends religious and cultural elements, often using Hebrew lyrics that convey spiritual and everyday themes.

Spiritual and Cultural Significance

- **Religious Rituals:** These melodies enhance religious rituals, adding a deep sense of spirituality to synagogue services, lifecycle events, and holidays.
- **Cultural Identity:** Yemenite Jewish music serves as a powerful symbol of cultural identity, preserving the traditions, language, and unique musical heritage of Yemenite Jews.
- **Expression of Faith:** The music allows individuals and communities to express their faith, joy, and connection to God.
- **Interplay of Traditions:** Yemenite Jewish music blends Jewish and Yemenite cultural traditions, creating a tapestry of sound that resonates with heritage and faith.

Yemenite Jewish music is a testament to the enduring strength of Yemenite Jewish communities, who have preserved their traditions and spirituality through the ages. It is a vibrant and cherished tradition that continues to enrich Jewish culture and spirituality, transcending time and place with its haunting melodies and cultural significance.

Sephardic Piyyutim: Poetry of the Soul

Sephardic Piyyutim are poetic expressions of Sephardic Jewish spirituality, encapsulating the profound connection between words, music, and devotion. These poetic compositions, often sung in Hebrew and Ladino, have been integral to Sephardic Jewish culture for centuries.

Poetry and Musical Elements

Sephardic Piyyutim are marked by their poetic depth and melodic richness, drawing on a vast reservoir of Jewish, Arabic, and Andalusian literary traditions.

- **Linguistic Diversity:** Piyyutim can be found in various languages, including Hebrew, Ladino, and Arabic, reflecting the diverse heritage of Sephardic communities.
- **Mystical Themes:** Many Piyyutim explore mystical themes, drawing from Kabbalistic and Sufi influences to create a sense of spiritual transcendence.
- **Instruments:** While some Piyyutim are performed as a cappella, others may incorporate traditional instruments such as the oud or violin, enhancing the music's cultural richness.
- **Harmony and Choral Singing:** Like Zemirot, Piyyutim is often sung harmoniously, fostering communal unity and spiritual elevation.

Religious and Cultural Significance

- **Liturgy:** These poetic compositions are often integrated into religious services, adding depth and emotion to prayers and rituals.
- **Cultural Heritage:** Piyyutim preserves Sephardic Jewish communities' linguistic and cultural heritage, reflecting their unique traditions and history.
- **Spiritual Journey:** For congregants, singing Piyyutim is a spiritual journey, allowing them to connect on a deeper level with the Divine.
- **Community Bonding:** Piyyutim brings communities together in song and celebration, fostering a sense of togetherness.

Sephardic Piyyutim bridges the gap between the earthly and the Divine through the power of words and melody, offering a glimpse into the rich culture of Sephardic Judaism, where language and music unite to create a profound spiritual experience.

Chasidic Nigunim: The Song of the Soul

Chasidic Nigunim is the transcendent melody of the Chasidic Jewish tradition. It's an embodiment of spiritual joy and connection. These wordless tunes elevate the soul, inspiring a deep devotion and unity among Chasidic communities.

Melodies and Musical Elements

Chasidic Nigunim are characterized by their simplicity, repetitive motifs, and emotional depth.

- **Soulful Repetition:** Nigunim often consists of short phrases or motifs repeated rhythmically. This repetition allows for deep immersion in the music and creates a meditative and ecstatic experience.
- **Harmonious Choral Singing:** Chasidic Nigunim is typically sung in groups, with congregants joining harmoniously. The collective voices create a powerful and spiritually resonant atmosphere.
- **Instrumentation:** While Nigunim is primarily vocal, traditional Chasidic instruments like the violin or accordion may accompany the singing, enriching the sonic landscape.
- **Emotional Expression:** These melodies convey emotions, from exuberant joy to heartfelt yearning, allowing worshippers to connect with their innermost feelings.

Spiritual and Communal Significance

- **Prayer and Meditation:** These melodies enhance the spiritual experience of prayer, facilitating a deep connection with the Divine.
- **Joy and Celebration:** Nigunim is often used in celebrations, especially during Chasidic weddings and festive gatherings, infusing the occasions with joy and devotion.
- **Communal Bonding:** Singing Nigunim as a community fosters a sense of unity, transcending individual boundaries and connecting worshippers on a spiritual level.
- **Spiritual Upliftment:** The repetitive and meditative quality of Nigunim has the power to elevate the soul, bringing worshippers to a heightened state of spiritual consciousness.

Chasidic Nigunim melodies inspire and uplift Chasidic Jewish communities worldwide, fostering a deep connection, devotion, and unity among the members.

Liturgical Chants: The Sacred Harmony of Jewish Worship

Liturgical chants, a cornerstone of Jewish worship, carry the weight of tradition and devotion in their melodies. These musical expressions have accompanied Jewish prayer for centuries. They provide a spiritual and meditative backdrop to communal and personal worship.

Melodies and Musical Elements

Liturgical chants encompass a wide range of melodies, each with its unique characteristics, but they share some common elements:

- **Hebrew Texts:** Liturgical chants are typically sung in Hebrew, the sacred language of Jewish prayer.

- **Cantillation Marks**: These musical notations, represented by specific symbols in the Hebrew text, guide scripture chanting and prayers in synagogue services.

- **Modality**: Chants often follow traditional modal scales, lending the music a timeless and reverent quality.

- **Solo and Congregational Singing:** Some liturgical chants are performed solo by a cantor, while others invite congregational participation, encouraging communal prayer.

Spiritual and Communal Significance

- **Enhancing Prayer:** Chanting scripture and prayers adds depth and emotion to the worship experience, allowing congregants to connect on a profound level with the sacred texts.

- **Meditation and Contemplation:** The repetitive nature of liturgical chants promotes meditation and contemplation, facilitating a spiritual journey during prayer.

- **Maintaining Tradition:** These chants preserve the timeless traditions of Jewish worship, connecting contemporary Jews with their historical and spiritual heritage.

- **Community Bonding:** Congregational singing of liturgical chants fosters a sense of unity and belonging within the synagogue community.

Liturgical chants are more than just music. They are a channel through which Jewish worshippers access their spirituality, connect with the Divine, and maintain a connection to their religious and cultural roots. Whether heard in a small synagogue or a grand temple, these chants continue to play a vital role in the spiritual life of Jewish communities worldwide.

Music is a powerful tool for spiritual connection and communal bonding. From the soulful melodies of Piyyutim and Chasidic Nigunim to the timeless chants of Jewish liturgy, music has been an integral part of Jewish worship for centuries. It enhances prayer, fosters unity, and helps carry on the traditions of our faith. Music brings people together, inspiring devotion and creating a bridge between the Divine and the earthly. Whether it's an ancient chant or a new musical expression, music will remain a crucial part of Jewish life for generations to come.

Chapter 7: Home and Family Tradition

Judaism treasures the family and home as core to its faith. Jewish homes are considered sacred spaces, where rituals like Passover Seder and Hanukkah menorah lighting are hosted. Parents bear the responsibility of passing down faith, values, and traditions. The home also serves as a place of prayer and reflection. In Judaism, the family and home are a big part of keeping their faith and culture alive from one generation to the next.

The Central Role of Home and Family in Jewish Culture and Religious Life

In Jewish culture and religious life, the home and family occupy a central and cherished position, shaping the essence of Jewish identity and practice. This profound connection between home and faith is deeply ingrained in the traditions and values of Judaism.

Home as a Sanctuary

Jewish homes are regarded as sacred spaces, mirroring the concept of the Mikdash Me'at, a miniature sanctuary. This sanctity is evident in the observance of rituals like the Passover Seder, where families come together to retell the story of the Exodus. Similarly, the Hanukkah menorah's lighting symbolizes the oil's miracle. These rituals are not confined to the synagogue but are integral to the Jewish home.

Family as the Foundation

Family is a cornerstone of religious life in Judaism.
https://www.pexels.com/photo/blond-baby-with-his-parents-4452209/

In Judaism, the family unit is the cornerstone of religious life. Parents play a pivotal role in passing down faith, values, and traditions to their children. Within the familial embrace, young generations learn about the ethical principles and customs that define Judaism. The home becomes a classroom where Jewish identity is nurtured.

A Hub for Spiritual Reflection

Beyond rituals, the home is a place of prayer and introspection. Daily prayers, meditation, and the observance of Shabbat, the weekly day of rest, often occur within the family setting. It creates a seamless connection between faith and daily life.

Welcoming the Stranger

Judaism strongly emphasizes hospitality and welcoming guests, known as Hachnasat Orchim. This practice reinforces the idea that the home is not just for family but a place of outreach and connection to the wider community. Welcoming strangers is seen as a sacred duty, embodying the values of kindness and inclusivity.

A Source of Continuity

The family-home connection is a wellspring of continuity in Jewish culture and religious life. It ensures that faith remains vibrant and traditions are preserved across generations. This continuity is vital for the survival and thriving of Jewish identity in a rapidly changing world.

The home and family in Judaism are not just physical spaces and relationships. They are spiritual anchors that infuse everyday life with meaning and purpose. They provide a nurturing environment in which Jewish traditions are sustained and celebrated, creating a legacy that endures from one generation to the next.

Shabbat Dinner: A Tapestry of Jewish Unity

Shabbat dinner, a beloved Jewish tradition, weaves warmth and continuity through generations. Rooted in the biblical commandment to observe the Sabbath, this ritual holds deep spiritual and cultural significance. It brings families and communities together in a sacred and heartwarming experience.

Origins and Significance

Shabbat dinner's origins date back to the Book of Genesis, where God sanctified the seventh day as a day of rest. Lighting the Shabbat candles and sharing a festive meal is a way to commemorate this Divine rest.

Observance Today

Shabbat dinner is a blend of tradition and personal touches:

- **Candle Lighting:** The woman of the house typically lights the Shabbat candles, ushering in the Sabbath's peace.
- **Kiddush:** Over a cup of wine, the Kiddush prayer sanctifies the Sabbath.
- **Challah:** A braided challah bread baked with love symbolizes abundance and unity.
- **Feast:** Shabbat dinners are festive, often with traditional dishes passed down through generations.

Shabbat dinner, in its diverse forms across Jewish communities worldwide, encapsulates the essence of Jewish life. It's a moment where time stands still, and the warmth of family and faith embraces all who gather around the table, creating lasting memories.

Kosher Kitchen Practices: Bridging Faith and Food

Kosher kitchen practices lie at the intersection of faith and nourishment. It reflects the bond between Jewish dietary laws and spiritual well-being. Rooted in ancient biblical commandments, these practices are a testament to the enduring commitment of Jewish communities worldwide to uphold the kosher way of life.

Origins and Significance

Kosher kitchen practices are firmly anchored in the Torah's dietary laws, outlining what is permissible (kosher) and what is not (non-kosher). These laws serve several vital purposes:

- **Spiritual Connection**: Adherence to kosher dietary laws fosters a spiritual connection between individuals and their faith by obeying God's commandments.
- **Cultural Identity**: Kosher practices are emblematic of Jewish identity, preserving a distinct cultural and religious heritage.
- **Holistic Health**: Kosher laws prioritize both physical and spiritual well-being. They ensure food is prepared cleanly and wholesomely, promoting health and holiness.

Observance Today

- **Kosher Animals:** Only specific animals, such as those with split hooves that chew their cud, are deemed kosher. Proper slaughtering techniques maintain the meat's kosher status.
- **Meat and Dairy Separation**: A fundamental principle is that meat and dairy products are never mixed. Separate utensils and cookware are used for each category, observing a waiting period between meat and dairy consumption.
- **Kosher Certification**: Many packaged foods bear a kosher certification symbol (hechsher), signifying compliance with kosher standards.
- **Blessings and Prayers**: Blessings before and after meals acknowledge God's role in providing sustenance, affirming the tradition of thanking the Creator.

David Levy says, *"In our kosher kitchen, I vividly remember my grandmother, Bubbe Esther, teaching me to separate dairy and meat, ensuring our meals were not just delicious but also infused with tradition."*

Kosher kitchen practices, while deeply traditional, continue to evolve with modernity. They ensure that dietary choices nurture the body as well as the soul. They help establish a profound connection to God, culture, and the global Jewish community.

Sukkah Building during Sukkot: Embracing the Divine Shelter

Sukkah building is a joyous and deeply symbolic tradition observed during the Jewish holiday of Sukkot. It is a tangible expression of Jewish faith, unity, and gratitude rooted in ancient agricultural practices and biblical commandments.

Origins and Significance

The practice of building sukkahs, temporary outdoor shelters, has its roots in the agricultural festivals of ancient Israel. Sukkot is a harvest festival, and during biblical times, people would dwell in sukkahs as they harvested their crops. It symbolized their dependence on God's bounty.

- **Divine Shelter:** Building and dwelling in a sukkah is a way of acknowledging God's protection and provision, much like the Divine shelter provided during the desert wanderings of the Israelites.

- **Unity and Hospitality:** The sukkah is a place of gathering where family and friends come together to share meals and celebrate. It promotes unity and hospitality, welcoming guests from all walks of life.

- **Transience:** Its impermanent nature serves as a reminder of life's transience and the need to appreciate the present moment.

Observance Today

Sukkah building is a hands-on, communal affair.

- **Construction:** Families and communities construct sukkahs in their yards or communal spaces. These temporary structures are made with wooden or metal frames covered by branches or thatch.

- **Decoration:** Sukkahs are adorned with fruits, vegetables, and artwork, creating a vibrant and festive atmosphere.

- **Dwelling and Meals:** Observant Jews eat their meals in the sukkah throughout the week of Sukkot, and some even sleep there, connecting with past traditions.

- **Wave the Lulav and Etrog:** During Sukkot, worshippers also perform the mitzvah (commandment) of waving the lulav (palm branch) and etrog (citron), symbols of the harvest.

Sukkah building during Sukkot is a tangible way for Jewish individuals and communities to connect with their heritage. It's a Divine way to express gratitude for life's blessings and embrace the value of hospitality. This tradition thrives, providing a space for reflection and communal bonding.

Bedtime Shema: A Nightly Ritual of Reflection and Protection

The Bedtime Shema is a cherished Jewish tradition that closes each day with a moment of reflection, gratitude, and protection. This nightly ritual, steeped in faith and spirituality, offers a sense of security and connection to God before sleep.

Origins and Significance

The Bedtime Shema is rooted in the Shema, one of the most fundamental Jewish prayers found in the Torah. The Shema proclaims the oneness of God and the commandment to love and serve Him with all one's heart, soul, and might. Its nighttime recitation extends this declaration into the realm of dreams and slumber. The significance of the Bedtime Shema lies in the following:

- **Faithful Acknowledgment**: It reaffirms one's faith in God and accepting His sovereignty, even as the day ends.
- **Protection:** The prayer is believed to provide spiritual protection during the vulnerable state of sleep, invoking God's presence to safeguard the soul.
- **Reflection and Gratitude**: The Bedtime Shema encourages reflection on one's actions throughout the day and expressions of gratitude for life's blessings.

Eliana Cohen says, *"Every night, I hold my child close, whispering the Shema softly. In that sacred moment, feeling their warmth, I'm connected to generations past as they drift off to sleep."*

Observance Today

- **Recitation:** Individuals recite the Shema and a series of blessings before sleeping. The Shema is often whispered or said in a hushed tone, emphasizing the quiet and contemplative nature of the ritual.

- **Covering the Eyes:** Some individuals cover their eyes with their hands as they recite the Shema, symbolizing their focus on the inner, spiritual world.
- **Personal Prayers:** After the recitation, many people offer personal prayers, expressing their thoughts, concerns, and hopes to God.

The Bedtime Shema is a bridge between the waking world and the realm of dreams. It allows Jewish individuals to sleep with peace, protection, and a deep connection to their faith. It is a tradition that has endured through generations, offering solace and spiritual nourishment in the quiet moments before slumber.

Hanukkah Candle Lighting: Kindling the Flames of Miracles

Hanukkah candle lighting commemorates the miraculous events of Hanukkah.
https://www.pexels.com/photo/person-lighting-menorah-3730975/

Hanukkah candle lighting, also known as the lighting of the menorah, is a beloved Jewish tradition that commemorates the miraculous events of Hanukkah. Rooted in a historical victory and a miracle that unfolded over two millennia ago, this ritual symbolizes hope, resilience, and the enduring light of faith.

Origins and Significance

Hanukkah commemorates the rededication of the Second Temple in Jerusalem after its desecration by the Seleucid Empire. The miracle at the heart of Hanukkah involves a small flask of oil, which should have lasted only one day but miraculously burned for eight days. The significance of Hanukkah candle lighting is multi-fold:

- **Miracle and Redemption:** The candles symbolize the miracle of the oil and the Jewish people's triumph over oppression, highlighting the resilience and faith that sustained them.

- **Publicizing the Miracle:** Jews are commanded to "publicize the miracle" by displaying the menorah in a window or other public place, spreading the message of hope and faith to all.

- **Family and Tradition:** Hanukkah is a time for families to unite, light the candles, and exchange gifts. It fosters a sense of unity and continuity.

Observance Today

- **The Menorah:** A nine-branched candelabrum called a menorah is used. Eight candles represent the eight days the oil burned, while the ninth, the shamash (helper), is used to light the others.

- **Progressive Lighting:** One candle is lit on the first night, two on the second, and so on until all eight candles are illuminated by the end of Hanukkah.

- **Blessings:** Special blessings are recited before and after lighting the candles, praising God for the miracles of Hanukkah.

- **Singing and Celebration:** Families often sing Hanukkah songs, exchange gifts, and enjoy festive foods like latkes (potato pancakes) and sufganiyot (jelly-filled donuts).

Hanukkah candle lighting reminds Jews of all ages that miracles can happen, even in times of darkness, and faith can overcome adversity. It is a tradition that continues to inspire the belief passed down from generation to generation.

Pesach (Passover) Seder: A Journey from Slavery to Freedom

The Pesach (Passover) Seder is a Jewish tradition that encapsulates the essence of the Passover holiday. It is a meticulously structured ceremonial meal that guides participants through the Exodus story, from slavery to liberation. It fosters a sense of history, faith, and identity.

Origins and Significance

The Passover Seder is rooted in the biblical narrative of the Israelites' enslavement in Egypt and their miraculous deliverance. It serves several vital purposes:

- **Historical Remembrance:** The Seder ensures that the memory of the Exodus is preserved, allowing each generation to feel as if they experienced the journey from bondage to freedom.

- **Educational Tool:** Through rituals, readings, and symbolic foods, the Seder is an educational tool. It teaches young and old about the significance of freedom and faith.

- **Covenant Renewal:** The Seder reinforces the covenant between God and the Jewish people. It emphasizes their "chosenness" and the Divine protection that led to liberation.

Observance Today

- **The Haggadah:** A guidebook called the Haggadah contains the order of the Seder, complete with the Exodus story, songs, blessings, and explanations.

- **The Seder Plate:** A special plate holds symbolic foods like matzah (unleavened bread), maror (bitter herbs), and lamb shank bone. Each represents different aspects of the Exodus story.

- **Four Cups of Wine:** Four cups of wine are consumed throughout the Seder, each symbolizing a promise from God.

- **Matzah:** The unleavened bread, or matzah, represents the haste with which the Israelites left Egypt, as there was no time for the bread to rise.

- **Afikomen:** A piece of matzah is hidden and later found by children, encouraging their active participation.

- **Discussion and Song:** The Seder includes questions, discussions, and songs that engage participants in retelling the Exodus story.

The Pesach Seder is a rich, immersive experience that brings Jewish families and communities together. It reaffirms the values of freedom, faith, and remembrance. It also ensures that the Exodus story remains a living, breathing part of Jewish identity, passed down from generation to generation.

Tu B'Shevat Seder: Celebrating the Renewal of Nature and Spirit

The Tu B'Shevat Seder is a unique and spiritually enriching Jewish tradition. It honors the environment, changing seasons, and the connection between humanity and the natural world. Rooted in ancient agricultural practices and revived by the Kabbalists in the 16th century, this celebration marks the "New Year for Trees."

Origins and Significance

Tu B'Shevat, occurring on the 15th day of the Hebrew month of Shevat, has biblical origins as a marker for tithing fruits grown in the Land of Israel. Over time, it evolved into a celebration of nature's renewal.

- **Environmental Awareness:** Tu B'Shevat encourages ecological consciousness and stewardship. It highlights Judaism's deep respect for the environment.
- **Spiritual Connection:** The Seder offers a unique opportunity for spiritual reflection, using fruits, trees, and their symbolism to connect with God and the world.
- **Kabbalistic Influence:** Kabbalists in Tzfat, Israel, developed the Tu B'Shevat Seder, using mystical elements to enhance the experience.

Observance Today

- **Four Cups of Wine or Juice:** Much like the Passover Seder, four cups are consumed, each representing a different spiritual growth and connection.
- **Fruits and Nuts:** Various fruits and nuts, both from the Land of Israel and around the world, are eaten in a specific order, symbolizing different levels of spiritual ascent.
- **Blessings and Readings:** Special blessings are recited for different types of fruits, and readings from the Bible and other sources explore the connection between nature and spirituality.

- **Songs and Discussion:** Participants engage in songs, discussions, and activities related to the environment, personal growth, and ethical living.

The Tu B'Shevat Seder is a reminder of the cyclical nature of the world and our role in preserving it. It fosters a deep appreciation for the environment, spirituality, and the interconnectedness of all living beings. In a world where environmental consciousness is increasingly critical, this tradition is a testament to Judaism's enduring commitment to faith and the Earth.

Rosh Hashanah Challah Baking: Welcoming the New Year with Sweetness

Rosh Hashanah Challah baking is a heartwarming Jewish tradition that combines the aroma of freshly baked bread with the sweetness of the New Year. This meaningful practice fills homes with the scent of love and tradition and symbolizes hope, unity, and the promise of a sweet year ahead.

Rosh Hashanah Challah baking combines the aroma of freshly baked bread with the New Year.
https://www.pexels.com/photo/close-up-photography-of-bread-1002322/

Origins and Significance

Rosh Hashanah, the Jewish New Year, is a time of reflection, introspection, and renewal. Enjoying sweet foods, such as apples dipped in honey, to usher in a year filled with blessings is customary. Challah, the braided bread traditionally eaten on Shabbat and holidays, takes on a special significance during Rosh Hashanah Challah baking:

- **Sweetness:** The Challah is sweetened with honey or raisins to symbolize the hope for a sweet and joyous year.
- **Circular Shape:** Some Challahs are shaped into circles, symbolizing the cycle of the year and the desire for a year filled with blessings without end.
- **Braiding:** The braiding of the Challah represents unity and togetherness within the community and the family.

Observance Today

- **Preparation:** Families gather to prepare the Challah dough, which often includes the addition of honey or raisins for sweetness.
- **Shaping:** The Challah is shaped, with some opting for a circular design. This creative process allows for personal expression and artistry.
- **Blessings:** Special blessings are recited during the preparation and baking, invoking God's blessings for the upcoming year.
- **Sharing:** The freshly baked Challah is shared with family and friends during the Rosh Hashanah meal.
- **Prayers and Reflection:** During the meal, prayers are recited, and families reflect on the past year and express their hopes for the year ahead.

Leah Cohen shares, "*My hands shape the challah, adding honey for sweetness. With each braid, I feel connected to countless generations who baked this symbolic bread, a tangible link to our heritage.*"

Rosh Hashanah Challah baking is a sensory and spiritual experience that brings families and communities together. It represents the desire for a blessed year ahead filled with love, growth, and gratitude.

Yom Kippur Breakfast: Nourishing the Soul after a Day of Atonement

The Yom Kippur Breakfast is a Jewish tradition that follows the solemn day of fasting and repentance. It is a moment of physical and spiritual nourishment where families and communities unite to break their fast and strengthen the bonds of love and forgiveness.

Origins and Significance

Yom Kippur, the Day of Atonement, is the holiest day in the Jewish calendar, marked by fasting and intense prayer. The Yom Kippur Breakfast holds several significant meanings:

- **Completing the Day:** After a day of self-reflection, prayer, and fasting, the meal symbolizes the end of Yom Kippur and a return to everyday life.
- **Renewal and Reconciliation:** Sharing a meal underscores the themes of forgiveness, reconciliation, and renewal central to Yom Kippur.
- **Community and Togetherness**: Breaking the fast with family and friends strengthens Jewish people's sense of community and unity.

Michael Goldstein shares, "*The first bite after a day of fasting tastes like a fresh start. Sharing this meal with my family, we seek forgiveness and promise to be better in the year ahead.*"

Observance Today

The Yom Kippur Breakfast is a poignant and meaningful tradition:

- **Light and Nourishing Foods**: The meal typically begins with light and easily digestible foods, such as challah, eggs, and dairy products.
- **Symbolic Foods**: Many incorporate round or sweet foods, like honey or bread, into the meal to symbolize the cycle of life and the hope for a sweet year ahead.
- **Blessings and Prayers**: Special blessings are recited over the food, expressing gratitude for sustenance and seeking blessings for the coming year.
- **Family and Community**: Families often gather at home, while some communities host communal Breakfast events, fostering a sense of togetherness.
- **Reflection and Sharing:** The meal provides an opportunity for loved ones to reflect on the day's prayers, seek forgiveness from one another, and share their hopes for the future.

The Yom Kippur Breakfast is more than a meal. It's a symbol of spiritual and emotional nourishment. It reinforces the values of forgiveness, unity, and the power of a fresh start. It's a reminder of the profound connection between your physical and spiritual selves.

Purim Costumes and Parties: Embracing Joy and Tradition

Purim costumes and parties are a vibrant and festive aspect of Jewish culture, celebrated during the joyous holiday of Purim. Colorful costumes, exuberant gatherings, and acts of charity characterize this tradition, capturing the spirit of Purim's message of triumph over adversity, unity, and unbridled happiness.

Origins and Significance

Purim commemorates the events described in the Book of Esther, where Queen Esther and her cousin Mordecai thwarted the evil Haman's plan to annihilate the Jewish people in ancient Persia. Purim costumes and parties hold several meanings:

- **Hidden Identities**: Purim's story contains hidden identities and concealed truths. Wearing costumes allows participants to mimic this theme.

- **Unity and Community**: Parties and gatherings promote unity within the Jewish community, fostering a sense of belonging and camaraderie.

- **Joy and Celebration:** Purim encourages unabashed joy and celebration, demonstrating the Jewish people's resilience and ability to find light even in the darkest of times.

Observance Today

- **Creative Costumes:** People of all ages dress in costumes, with children often emulating their favorite Purim characters. Costume creativity, ranging from biblical figures to modern pop culture icons, knows no bounds.

- **Charitable Acts**: On Purim, Jews perform acts of charity (tzedakah) by giving to those in need, ensuring that all can join the festivities.

- **Mishloach Manot**: It's customary to exchange Purim gift baskets filled with sweets and treats with family and friends.

- **Megillah Reading**: The Book of Esther, known as the Megillah, is read aloud in synagogues, recounting the miraculous events of Purim.

- **Feasting and Merriment:** Purim parties often include feasting, music, dancing, and the retelling of the Purim story.

Purim costumes and parties encapsulate the holiday's core value of triumph of good over evil. These celebrations honor the past and allow individuals and communities to come together in jubilant revelry. It strengthens bonds and embodies the resilience of the Jewish spirit.

Lag B'Omer Bonfires: Illuminating Jewish Unity and Resilience

Lag B'Omer bonfires are a captivating Jewish tradition celebrated on the 33rd day of the Omer, a period of semi-mourning between Passover and Shavuot. This tradition involves lighting bonfires, creating a luminous spectacle, and symbolizing Jewish unity, spiritual growth, and historical resilience.

Origins and Significance

- **Bar Yochai:** Lag B'Omer is associated with the passing of Rabbi Shimon Bar Yochai, a revered sage and author of the Zohar, a foundational text of Jewish mysticism (Kabbalah).

- **Ceasing of Plague:** According to tradition, a plague that had afflicted Rabbi Akiva's students ceased on this day, signifying a time of relief and spiritual reawakening.

- **Bar Yochai's Revelation:** Rabbi Shimon Bar Yochai revealed the inner teachings of the Torah, emphasizing the mystical aspects of Judaism.

Observance Today

- **Bonfires:** Communities gather to light bonfires, often featuring towering flames. Each fire represents the illumination of Jewish spirituality and unity.

- **Song and Dance:** People sing and dance around the bonfires, creating a joyful and spirited atmosphere.

- **Haircuts:** It is customary for children to receive their first haircuts on Lag B'Omer, known as an "Upsherin" in Yiddish, symbolizing the beginning of their Jewish education.

- **Archery and Picnics:** Recreational activities, such as archery and picnics, are enjoyed in a spirit of togetherness.

- **Spiritual Reflection**: Lag B'Omer serves as a time for introspection and personal growth, with people using the occasion to focus on spiritual improvement.

Lag B'Omer bonfires commemorate historical events and emphasize the resilience of the Jewish people and the enduring quest for spiritual enlightenment. These gatherings foster a sense of unity and community. They encourage individuals to embrace their unique spiritual journeys while celebrating their shared heritage.

Home and family traditions are deeply embedded within Jewish culture, reflecting the spiritual values of faith, togetherness, and resilience. Whether it's gathering around a festive breakfast table on Yom Kippur or celebrating joyfully with costumes and bonfires on Purim and Lag B'Omer, these customs offer an opportunity to cultivate meaningful connections with yourself, your loved ones, and your community.

Chapter 8: Learning, Wisdom, and Academia

Jewish learning is a treasure chest of wisdom that spans thousands of years. Jews have a deep love for learning, believing that gaining wisdom is a lifelong journey. In Jewish tradition, study is highly respected, and scholars are honored. They have special places for learning called yeshivas and synagogues, where people gather to study the Torah, Talmud, and other sacred texts. These texts contain religious teachings and lessons about life, ethics, and how to be a good person.

Today, Jewish academia extends beyond religious texts. Jewish scholars, known as rabbis, have shared their insights on various topics, from law and ethics to science and philosophy. Jews have significantly contributed to medicine, mathematics, literature, and the arts. This love for learning has helped them thrive and positively impact the world. In Jewish culture, pursuing knowledge is a way to connect with the Divine and improve the world. It's a reminder that learning never stops, and wisdom is a treasure that grows brighter with time.

The Role and Importance of Learning in Judaism

Learning has always been at the core of Jewish tradition, and its importance can be traced back to the very origins of Judaism. The sacred texts, particularly the Torah, emphasize the value of knowledge and command Jews to study and seek wisdom continually. This commitment to learning has been a guiding principle in Jewish life for millennia.

The Torah: The Source of Wisdom

The Torah is the foundational text of Judaism.
https://www.pexels.com/photo/person-reading-a-book-4034445/

The Torah, the foundational text of Judaism, is revered as the Divine instruction manual for living a righteous and meaningful life. It contains laws and commandments intertwined with narratives, poetry, and profound ethical teachings. Jewish learning begins with Torah study, considered a source of unparalleled wisdom and guidance.

The Commandment to Study (Talmud Torah)

Judaism emphasizes the commandment of the Talmud Torah, which obligates Jews to study and teach the Torah. This commandment is derived from passages in the Torah, such as Deuteronomy 6:7, which instructs, "*You shall teach [the words of God] diligently to your children.*" This Divine injunction underscores the centrality of learning within the Jewish faith.

Lifelong Learning and Intellectual Exploration

Judaism views learning as a lifelong journey. The Talmud, a central Jewish law and ethics text, encourages continuous study, asserting that "*study is great because it leads to action*" (Talmud, Kiddushin 40b). Jews are encouraged to engage in intellectual exploration, debate, and discussion, believing that the quest for understanding is a pathway to spiritual growth and ethical living.

Scholars and teachers, known as rabbis, play a pivotal role in Jewish communities. They dedicate their lives to the study of sacred texts and the interpretation of Jewish law. Rabbis guide congregants in matters of faith, ethics, and ritual observance. They ensure that the wisdom of the Torah is transmitted effectively.

Torah Study: Unveiling the Wisdom of Jewish Tradition

The tradition of Torah study is at the heart of Jewish intellectual and spiritual life, dating back millennia. At its core is the Torah, the central and most sacred text in Judaism, which includes the Five Books of Moses, also known as the Pentateuch.

Origins and Importance

Torah study began with the Jewish people's earliest encounters with this sacred text. It's rooted in the belief that the Torah contains the written law and a vast reservoir of wisdom, guidance, and moral teachings. Torah encompasses the history, ethics, theology, and legal principles that form the bedrock of Jewish identity.

Practices Today

Torah study has evolved, reflecting the diversity of Jewish communities and their interpretations of this ancient text. Here's how it's practiced today:

- **Yeshivot and Seminaries:** Traditional Jewish academies, known as yeshivot for men and seminaries for women, offer intensive Torah study programs. Students delve deep into Jewish texts, including the Talmud and commentaries.

- **Weekly Torah Portions:** In synagogues worldwide, Jews gather weekly to study the Torah portion (parashah) assigned for that week. This practice ensures that the entire Torah is read and studied over a year.

- **Chevruta Study:** Partnered Torah study (chevruta) is a cherished tradition. Two individuals explore texts together, engaging in lively debates and discussions to gain a deeper understanding.

- **Online Resources:** In the digital age, Torah study is accessible globally through websites, podcasts, and online courses. These

resources cater to Jews of all backgrounds and levels of expertise.
- **Daily Study**: Many Jews dedicate time each day to study a page of the Talmud, known as Daf Yomi. This seven-and-a-half-year cycle ensures a comprehensive exploration of the Talmud.
- **Application to Modern Life**: Torah study isn't solely an intellectual pursuit. It's also a guide for ethical living. Lessons from the Torah inform ethics, justice, and social responsibility decisions.

Torah study serves as a cornerstone of Jewish identity, fostering a deep connection to tradition, a sense of shared heritage, and a commitment to lifelong learning. It empowers individuals to apply timeless wisdom to contemporary challenges. Torah study remains a vibrant and essential aspect of Jewish life, preserving the enduring legacy of Jewish scholarship and spirituality.

Talmud Study: The Heart of Jewish Scholarship

The Talmud is a central text of rabbinic Judaism.
Reuvenk, CC BY 3.0 <https://creativecommons.org/licenses/by/3.0>, via Wikimedia Commons: https://commons.wikimedia.org/wiki/File:Talmud_set.JPG

Talmud study is the cornerstone of Jewish scholarship, fostering intellectual rigor, ethical insight, and a profound understanding of Jewish law and tradition. It is an intricate exploration of the Talmud, a central text of rabbinic Judaism.

Origins

The Talmud is a compilation of Jewish oral law and traditions developed over centuries. Its origins trace back to the Second Temple period, but it was primarily codified in the Babylonian and Jerusalem Talmuds. Talmud study emerged as a response to the need for a comprehensive Jewish law and ethics guide.

Importance

- **Legal Foundation:** It serves as the foundation of Jewish law (Halakha) and provides extensive commentary on biblical texts.
- **Intellectual Challenge:** Talmudic discourse encourages critical thinking, debate, and intellectual exploration, nurturing analytical minds.
- **Ethical Guidance:** The Talmud imparts ethical wisdom, offering guidance on moral dilemmas, interpersonal relationships, and social justice.

Practices Today

- **Yeshivot:** Specialized institutions, known as yeshivot, offer comprehensive Talmudic education for scholars and students.
- **Daf Yomi:** The global Daf Yomi program unites Jews worldwide in daily Talmud study, completing the entire Talmudic cycle every seven and a half years.
- **Online Resources:** Digital platforms provide access to Talmudic texts, commentaries, and lectures, enabling widespread engagement.
- **Community Classes:** Many synagogues and community centers offer Talmud study groups, making them accessible to a broader audience.

Talmud study remains a dynamic and essential component of Jewish life, fostering intellectual growth, moral clarity, and a profound connection to Jewish heritage. It embodies the spirit of continuous inquiry and reflection that has defined Jewish scholarship for centuries.

Yeshiva Learning: Nurturing Torah Scholars

Yeshiva learning is the heart of Jewish education, where students engage in deep, immersive study of Torah, Talmud, and Jewish law. These specialized schools foster a lifelong love of learning and prepare individuals for roles as scholars, teachers, and leaders in the Jewish community.

Origins

The concept of the yeshiva dates back to ancient times when scholars gathered to study Jewish texts. Over the centuries, yeshivot evolved into formal institutions with a structured curriculum. The term "*yeshiva*" itself means "sitting" in Hebrew, reflecting the traditional method of sitting and learning.

Importance

- **Preservation of Tradition:** It safeguards the continuity of Jewish tradition, ensuring that Torah and Talmudic scholarship remain vibrant and relevant.
- **Intellectual Depth:** Yeshivot provides a rigorous and comprehensive education, fostering deep intellectual engagement with Jewish texts and values.
- **Leadership Development:** Many Jewish leaders, rabbis, and educators emerge from yeshiva programs, shaping the future of Jewish communities worldwide.

Practices Today

- **Full-Time Study:** Yeshiva students dedicate themselves to full-time study, immersing in sacred texts and rabbinic commentaries.
- **Curriculum**: The curriculum includes Bible, Talmud, Jewish law, philosophy, and ethics, providing a well-rounded education.
- **Discourse and Debate**: Yeshiva learning encourages lively discourse, debate, and critical thinking, nurturing the skills needed for the interpretation and application of Jewish law.
- **Global Reach**: Yeshivot exists in Jewish communities worldwide, from Jerusalem to New York, offering diverse approaches to Jewish learning.

Yeshiva learning produces generations of scholars and leaders who carry the torch of Jewish wisdom, ensuring its vitality for years to come.

Midrash Study: Unveiling the Depths of Jewish Scripture

Midrash study is a profound exploration of Jewish scripture.
The National Library of Israel Collection, Public domain, via Wikimedia Commons:
https://commons.wikimedia.org/wiki/File:Midrash_Tehillim_(79).jpg

Midrash study is a profound exploration of Jewish scripture, uncovering layers of meaning and interpretation within the Bible's narratives and teachings. It's a bridge between the ancient text and contemporary understanding, inviting us to delve into Judaism's moral, spiritual, and ethical dimensions.

Origins

Midrashic interpretation has deep roots in Jewish tradition, emerging in the Second Temple period and flourishing in rabbinic literature. It seeks to fill in gaps, offer moral lessons, and extract hidden wisdom from biblical stories. Midrashim (plural) are collections of these interpretations.

Importance

- **Moral and Ethical Insight**: Midrashim reveals moral lessons and ethical insights embedded in biblical narratives, guiding individuals in their daily lives.

- **Understanding God's Will**: Helps Jews understand God's will and relate to Divine teachings meaningfully.

- **Cultural Continuity:** Midrashim contributes to the cultural continuity of Judaism, ensuring that the Bible remains a living text relevant to contemporary concerns.

Practices Today
- **Textual Exploration:** Scholars and students engage in deep textual analysis, examining Midrashim and their commentaries.
- **Educational Programs:** Many Jewish educational institutions incorporate Midrash study into their curriculum, fostering a deeper understanding of scripture.
- **Community Discussions:** Synagogues and study groups convene to discuss Midrashim, encouraging collective exploration and dialogue.
- **Online Resources:** Digital platforms provide access to a wealth of Midrashic literature, making it accessible to a wider audience.

Midrash study bridges the gap between ancient texts and contemporary life, offering insights into Judaism's moral, spiritual, and ethical dimensions. It keeps the flame of Jewish wisdom burning bright, ensuring that the timeless lessons of the Bible.

Jewish Philosophy: Navigating the Depths of Faith and Reason

Jewish philosophy is a rich intellectual tradition that combines faith and reason to explore profound questions about the nature of God, the meaning of life, and the ethical foundations of Judaism. Rooted in ancient texts, it continues to shape Judaism's spiritual and intellectual landscape.

Origins

Jewish philosophy has deep historical roots, with key figures like Philo of Alexandria and Maimonides blending Jewish thought with Greek and Islamic philosophy. These thinkers sought to reconcile the Jewish faith with the rational inquiries of the wider world, giving birth to a tradition of philosophical inquiry.

Importance
- **Theology and Metaphysics:** It grapples with questions about God's nature, theodicy, and the afterlife, contributing to theological understanding.

- **Ethics and Morality**: Jewish philosophers explore the ethical principles underlying Jewish law, shedding light on how to live a righteous life.
- **Interfaith Dialogue:** It has enriched interfaith dialogue by engaging with other philosophical traditions, fostering mutual understanding.

Practices Today

- **Academic Pursuit:** Scholars and students study the works of historical figures like Maimonides and modern philosophers like Emmanuel Levinas.
- **Ethical Reflection**: Jewish philosophy informs discussions on contemporary ethical challenges, such as bioethics, social justice, and environmental ethics.
- **Interdisciplinary Exploration**: It intersects with other fields, such as literature, theology, and political theory, enriching a broader discourse.
- **Interfaith Engagement:** Jewish philosophers engage in interfaith dialogue, contributing to religious pluralism and coexistence discussions.

Jewish philosophy inspires profound contemplation and dialogue, bridging the realms of faith and reason. It invites individuals to explore the depths of Jewish thought while engaging with the broader tapestry of human knowledge and ethics.

Kabbalah Study: Mystical Exploration of Jewish Spirituality

Kabbalah study delves into the mystical and esoteric dimensions of Jewish spirituality. It offers a unique path to understanding the relationship between the Divine, the cosmos, and the human soul, blending ancient wisdom with mystical insights.

Origins

Kabbalah has ancient origins but gained prominence in medieval Spain and later in Safed, Israel. Its teachings are rooted in texts like the Zohar and Sefer Yetzirah, offering a mystical interpretation of the Torah.

Importance
- **Spiritual Enlightenment:** Provides a framework for spiritual growth to deepen one's connection with God and the Divine realm.
- **Cosmic Understanding:** Kabbalistic teachings explore the creation of the universe and the interconnectedness of all existence.
- **Ethical Insights:** Kabbalah imparts ethical and moral guidance, encouraging individuals to live with compassion and empathy.

Practices Today
- **Textual Exploration:** Scholars and enthusiasts study Kabbalistic texts, deciphering their symbolic language and hidden meanings.
- **Meditation and Contemplation:** Kabbalah incorporates meditative practices to facilitate a direct encounter with the Divine.
- **Spiritual Retreats:** Some engage in Kabbalistic retreats or study groups, fostering a communal exploration of mystical teachings.
- **Contemporary Applications:** Kabbalah influences contemporary spirituality, with some seeking its wisdom for personal growth and enlightenment.

Kabbalah study offers a transformative journey into the mystical dimensions of Judaism, inviting individuals to explore the hidden aspects of reality, spirituality, and the human soul. It continues to spark spiritual quests and deepen the spiritual lives of those who seek its wisdom.

Jewish Mysticism: Navigating the Secrets of the Divine

Jewish mysticism, often called "Kabbalah," explores the hidden dimensions of reality and the Divine. It is a spiritual journey that seeks to fathom the mysteries of existence and the interconnectedness of all things.

Origins

Jewish mysticism traces its origins to antiquity but flourished during the Middle Ages, particularly in the writings of figures like Rabbi Isaac Luria and the Zohar. It draws on ancient Jewish texts, such as the Torah, while incorporating Neoplatonism and Gnostic thought elements.

Importance

- **Spiritual Connection:** Offers a direct and intimate connection with the Divine, allowing practitioners to experience deeper spirituality.
- **Cosmic Understanding:** Mysticism explores the nature of the universe, viewing it as a reflection of the Divine realm and unveiling hidden layers of reality.
- **Ethical Insight:** It emphasizes ethical behavior, encouraging individuals to embody compassion, kindness, and empathy.

Practices Today

- **Study of Kabbalistic Texts:** Scholars and enthusiasts study classic Kabbalistic texts like the Zohar and Sefer Yetzirah, decoding their symbolism and metaphysical teachings.
- **Meditation and Contemplation:** Mystical practices, including meditation and contemplation, enable individuals to access higher spiritual realms and Divine insights.
- **Kabbalah Centers:** Some engage with contemporary Kabbalah centers and study groups, applying mystical principles to modern life.
- **Artistic Expression:** Jewish mysticism has influenced art, literature, and music, providing a wellspring of inspiration for creative expression.

Jewish mysticism invites individuals to explore the mysteries of existence, deepen their connection with the Divine, and seek enlightenment and ethical living in a complex world. It remains a spiritual nourishment and wonder for those who embark on this mystical journey.

Liturgical Poetry: Elevating Prayer through Artistry

Liturgical poetry, also known as *piyyutim* in Hebrew, is a captivating expression that infuses Jewish prayer with artistic beauty and spiritual depth. These poetic compositions, often recited during religious services, enhance the worship experience by adding a layer of aesthetic richness to the liturgy.

Origins

The origins of liturgical poetry can be traced back to the Second Temple period when poets and sages crafted verses to accompany the rituals and festivals. Over time, these poems evolved, reflecting the diverse influences of Jewish communities across the diaspora.

Importance

- **Spiritual Elevation:** Piyyutim elevates prayer, allowing worshippers to connect with the Divine on an emotional and intellectual level.
- **Preserving Tradition:** These poems preserve Jewish communities' cultural and religious traditions, carrying the voices of generations.
- **Educational Tool:** Piyyutim conveys theological, historical, and moral lessons, serving as educational tools within the liturgy.

Practices Today

- **Recitation:** Piyyutim is recited during special occasions, holidays, and specific prayer services, enriching the liturgical experience.
- **Compositions:** Contemporary poets continue to compose piyyutim, contributing to the ongoing tradition of liturgical poetry.
- **Music and Melody:** Many piyyutim are set to melodies, enhancing their impact and fostering communal engagement.
- **Interpretation:** Scholars and enthusiasts delve into the interpretation and analysis of piyyutim, uncovering their layers of meaning.

Liturgical poetry is a testament to Judaism's enduring marriage of artistry and spirituality. These poetic expressions invite individuals to explore the depths of faith, celebrate the richness of tradition, and find inspiration in the intersection of words and worship.

Jewish Art and Musicology: Exploring the Creative Expression of Faith

Jewish art and musicology encompass a vibrant and diverse world of creative expression deeply rooted in Jewish tradition. These disciplines offer a lens through which to view the diverse Jewish culture, history, and spirituality, manifesting the beauty of faith through visual and auditory forms.

Origins

The origins of Jewish art and musicology can be traced to biblical times. Jewish art encompasses multiple styles and influences, including the illuminated manuscripts of medieval Spain. Jewish musicology explores the musical traditions of Ashkenazi and Sephardic Jews, among others.

Importance

- **Cultural Preservation:** They serve as vital tools for preserving Jewish culture and identity, reflecting the experiences and aesthetics of Jewish communities across the ages.

- **Spiritual Enrichment:** Jewish art and music provide pathways for spiritual enrichment, enhancing religious rituals and prayer services.

- **Interfaith Dialogue:** These disciplines foster interfaith dialogue by showcasing the shared human experience and the universal themes embedded in Jewish art and music.

Practices Today

- **Exhibitions and Performances:** Museums and cultural institutions host exhibitions of Jewish art while musicians and composers continue to create and perform Jewish music.

- **Academic Exploration:** Scholars and students engage in rigorous academic studies, dissecting the historical, cultural, and religious significance of Jewish artistic and musical expressions.

- **Inspirational Resources:** Jewish art and music are inspirations for individuals and communities, connecting them to their heritage and spirituality.

- **Interdisciplinary Collaboration:** Artists, musicians, and scholars often collaborate across disciplines, breathing new life into traditional forms and reimagining Jewish creative expression for contemporary audiences.

Jewish art and musicology continue to inspire, educate, and connect people worldwide, celebrating the enduring legacy of Jewish creativity and spirituality.

Responsa Literature: Navigating the Nuances of Jewish Law

Responsa literature, known as "She'elot u-Teshuvot" in Hebrew, addresses questions of Jewish law and ethics. This extensive body of written responses offers insights into the complexities of applying Jewish legal principles to real-life situations.

Origins

Responsa literature has its roots in the rabbinic tradition, with the earliest recorded responses dating back to the Geonic period. Over time, it expanded in scope and depth, reflecting the evolving needs of Jewish communities.

Importance

- **Legal Guidance:** It provides authoritative answers to questions that arise in daily life, offering practical solutions rooted in Jewish law.

- **Adaptation to Modernity:** Addresses contemporary issues, demonstrating Judaism's adaptability while maintaining its core values.

- **Preservation of Tradition:** Safeguards the continuity of Jewish legal tradition by documenting the application of Jewish law across centuries.

Practices Today

- **Rabbinic Authorities:** Contemporary rabbis and scholars engage in responsa writing, addressing modern legal and ethical dilemmas.

- **Halakhic Decisions:** Responsa shape halakhic decisions in various Jewish denominations, from Orthodox to Reform.

- **Interfaith Dialogues:** They contribute to interfaith discussions by showcasing the complexity and adaptability of Jewish law.

- **Scholarly Study:** Academics and students delve into responsa literature, examining its historical, cultural, and legal significance.

Responsa literature embodies the dynamism of Jewish law and ethics, offering a nuanced perspective on how Judaism guides individuals and communities in navigating the ever-evolving challenges of contemporary life. It continues to serve as a wellspring of wisdom and ethical insights for those seeking guidance within the framework of Jewish tradition.

Learning and wisdom are essential components of the Jewish faith and manifest in various forms. Judaism offers countless opportunities for intellectual exploration, spiritual enrichment, and intercultural dialogue, from liturgical poetry and musicology to responsa literature. Individuals cultivate an appreciation for the richness of Jewish tradition and its relevance to modern life by engaging with these disciplines. Ultimately, learning, wisdom, and academia remain at the core of Jewish faith and identity.

Chapter 9: Art and Creativity

Jewish art and creativity reflect the rich history and traditions of Jewish people. It's a diverse world of artistic expression, including painting, music, literature, and much more. Artists often draw inspiration from Jewish stories, history, and beliefs and use their creativity to explore what it means to be Jewish.

In visual art, Jewish artists create beautiful paintings, sculptures, and intricate designs for synagogues. They use symbols like the Star of David or Hebrew letters to express their faith. In music, Jewish composers have made significant contributions to classical, folk, and contemporary genres. Klezmer music, for example, is a lively and expressive form of Jewish folk music.

Jewish literature has produced renowned writers like Franz Kafka and Isaac Bashevis Singer, who explore themes of identity and belonging. Their stories resonate with readers worldwide. Jewish creativity also shines in cuisine, with dishes like matzah ball soup and latkes becoming popular Jewish foods.

Jewish art and creativity are vibrant and dynamic, reflecting Jewish culture's diversity and enduring spirit. They connect the past with the present, allowing Jewish people to express their identity and share their heritage through various forms of artistic expression.

Jewish Calligraphy (Sofer): Where Faith Meets Artistry

Jewish calligraphy melds written words into art.
Ishpashout, CC BY 3.0 <https://creativecommons.org/licenses/by/3.0>, via Wikimedia Commons: https://commons.wikimedia.org/wiki/File:Aeish-sheli.jpg

Jewish calligraphy, or "Sofer," is a tradition that melds the written word into a form of art deeply rooted in Jewish culture and faith. It brings the beauty of Hebrew script to life, weaving together language, spirituality, and artistic expression.

Historical Context

The origins of Jewish calligraphy trace back to ancient times, with the evolution of Hebrew script spanning centuries. Jewish communities in the diaspora encountered many cultures, from Arabic to European, influencing their calligraphic styles. Notably, the Sephardic and Ashkenazi scripts showcase this cross-cultural exchange.

Cultural Significance

Jewish calligraphy holds profound cultural significance. It is a tangible link to Jewish history, preserving the visual heritage of ancient manuscripts and Torah scrolls. This artistry enhances the spiritual experience, emotionally resonating prayer and sacred texts. Furthermore, it mirrors the rich interplay of cultures in Jewish history, where diverse influences converged, giving birth to a unique and enduring artistic tradition.

Practices Today

- **Torah Scrolls:** Sofrim (scribes) painstakingly write and restore Torah scrolls, ensuring their accuracy and artistic splendor.
- **Religious Art:** Calligraphers create religious artworks like ketubot (marriage contracts) and mezuzot, blending tradition with contemporary aesthetics.
- **Educational Endeavors:** Workshops and educational programs pass down the art of Jewish calligraphy to new generations.
- **Interfaith Exchange:** Jewish calligraphy engages in interfaith dialogue, inviting people from all backgrounds to appreciate its beauty and spirituality.

Jewish calligraphy beautifully bridges the past and the present, demonstrating the enduring vitality of Jewish culture. It showcases how art can bear the weight of history, faith, and creativity. It stands as a testament to the resilience and adaptability of Jewish tradition.

Synagogue Architecture: Where Spirituality Meets Design

Synagogue architecture is a captivating tradition that weaves faith, culture, and aesthetics together. It provides a sacred space where Jewish communities gather for worship and community and showcases the fusion of spiritual reverence with architectural innovation.

Synagogue architecture weaves faith, culture, and aesthetics together.
Uoaei1, CC BY-SA 4.0 <https://creativecommons.org/licenses/by-sa/4.0>, via Wikimedia Commons: https://commons.wikimedia.org/wiki/File:Praha_Spanish_Synagogue_Interior_01.jpg

Historical Context

The roots of synagogue architecture stretch back through centuries, reflecting the diverse cultural influences encountered by Jewish communities in the diaspora. Architectural styles have evolved from the ancient synagogues of the Roman period to the grandeur of Moorish and Gothic synagogues.

Cultural Significance

Synagogue architecture carries profound cultural significance. It serves as a tangible embodiment of Jewish identity. It offers a space for generations to celebrate, mourn, learn, and connect with their faith. Architectural elements, from the ark containing the Torah scrolls to the stained-glass windows, carry deep symbolism and artistic beauty.

Practices Today

- **Innovative Design:** Contemporary architects blend traditional elements with modern design, creating functional and spiritually uplifting spaces.
- **Preservation:** Restoration efforts ensure the preservation of historical synagogues, maintaining their cultural and architectural heritage.
- **Interfaith Dialogue:** Synagogue architecture fosters interfaith understanding, inviting diverse communities to appreciate its beauty and spirituality.
- **Educational Initiatives:** Educational programs and tours introduce people to synagogue architecture's rich history and symbolism.

Synagogue architecture beautifully melds the spiritual and the aesthetic. It showcases the enduring vitality of Jewish culture and faith. It stands as a testament to the resilience and adaptability of Jewish tradition, providing a sacred space where past, present, and future generations gather in reverence and community.

Jewish Folk Art (Including Paper Cutting): Tradition, Symbolism, and Artistry

Jewish folk art, a multifaceted reflection of Jewish culture, encompasses a variety of creative expressions. Among them, paper cutting is a harmonious blend of tradition, symbolism, and artistic innovation.

Historical Context

Jewish folk art has evolved, shaped by the experiences of Jewish communities worldwide. As Jews settled in different regions, their art absorbed local influences while retaining distinct Jewish themes. Paper cutting, for instance, reflects the delicate craftsmanship that thrived in Eastern European Jewish communities.

Cultural Significance

Jewish folk art is culturally significant, serving as a living repository of Jewish heritage. It captures the stories, values, and rituals that have shaped Jewish life for generations. Folk artists infuse their creations with symbolism, transforming everyday objects into visually captivating pieces. Beyond aesthetics, folk art reinforces Jewish identity, providing a visual language that transcends words.

Practices Today

- **Artistic Revival:** Modern artists draw inspiration from traditional Jewish folk art, infusing it with contemporary flair and fresh perspectives.
- **Cultural Education:** Educational programs and exhibitions introduce audiences to the rich history and symbolism embedded in Jewish folk art, fostering an appreciation for its cultural depth.
- **Interplay with Other Forms:** Folk art interacts with other artistic disciplines, enhancing Jewish creativity and contributing to broader cultural dialogues.
- **Community Bonding:** The creation of folk art frequently brings communities together, nurturing a sense of shared culture and tradition.

Jewish folk art beautifully marries artistic expression with tradition and bridges the past and present while adding vivid strokes to the ever-evolving canvas of Jewish identity.

Klezmer Music: The Soulful Sounds of Jewish Heritage

Klezmer music, an evocative and spirited genre, embodies the essence of Jewish culture, resonating with joy, sorrow, and the indomitable spirit of the Jewish people.

Historical Context

Klezmer music finds its roots in Jewish history, originating in Eastern Europe. It emerged as a harmonious blend of Jewish and Eastern European musical traditions, heavily influenced by Yiddish culture. Over time, it evolved as a response to the Jewish diaspora and accompanied pivotal life moments, from weddings to funerals.

Cultural Significance

Klezmer's music carries profound cultural significance. Klezmer musicians skillfully express a range of emotions through their instruments, from the exuberance of celebration to the poignant depths of reflection. This music serves as a vessel for preserving Jewish heritage and storytelling. Each Klezmer melody carries narratives of Jewish life, connecting generations. Moreover, Klezmer transcends language barriers.

It unites people through its emotive melodies, creating a sense of community and shared experience.

Practices Today

- **Revival:** Modern musicians infuse Klezmer with new life, offering fresh interpretations while respecting its traditional roots.
- **Cultural Education:** Workshops and festivals introduce new generations to Klezmer's rich heritage, ensuring its melodies and stories endure.
- **Interfaith Harmony:** Klezmer's captivating rhythms and melodies foster interfaith dialogue, building bridges between diverse communities.
- **Life Celebrations:** Klezmer continues to enrich Jewish weddings and celebrations, creating an atmosphere of unity and festivity.

Klezmer's music, with its timeless melodies and profound emotional depth, is a testament to Jewish culture's resilience. This musical tradition embraces heritage and innovation, inviting people of all backgrounds to immerse themselves in the vibrant sounds of Jewish history and identity.

Jewish Dance Forms: Celebrating Life's Rhythms

Jewish dance forms, a captivating expression of Jewish culture, encapsulate the rhythm of life's celebrations, from joyous weddings to spirited festivals.

Historical Context

These dance forms have deep historical roots, with origins spanning Jewish communities across the globe. They often reflect the influence of local cultures while maintaining a distinct Jewish identity. The dances evolved as a response to Jewish experiences in different regions, becoming an integral part of Jewish life.

Cultural Significance

Jewish dance forms hold profound cultural significance. Dance serves as a living embodiment of Jewish traditions. It captures the exuberance of celebration and the solemnity of reflection. It also brings shared experiences, preserving stories and memories across generations. Dance has a unifying power, fostering community and reinforcing Jewish identity.

Practices Today

- **Evolution**: Modern interpretations and innovations keep Jewish dance forms vibrant and relevant.
- **Cultural Education**: Dance workshops and festivals introduce new generations to these traditions, ensuring their legacy endures.
- **Inclusivity:** Jewish dance forms often transcend religious boundaries, promoting interfaith dialogue and cultural exchange.
- **Life's Milestones**: These dances enrich Jewish life events, infusing them with energy and a deep connection to tradition.

With their infectious rhythms and cultural resonance, Jewish dance forms invite people of all backgrounds to partake in the vibrant expressions of Jewish history and identity.

Jewish Painting and Sculpture: Capturing the Jewish Soul in Art

Jewish painting and sculpture, a captivating realm of artistic expression, serve as a canvas for exploring the diverse facets of Jewish identity and history.

Historical Context

This form of artistic expression finds its roots in Jewish communities worldwide. It reflects a tapestry of influences, from the ancient Hebrew artistic traditions to the multicultural exchanges in the diaspora. Jewish artists have drawn inspiration from their surroundings while infusing their works with Jewish themes.

Cultural Significance

Through strokes of a brush and tangible forms, these artworks preserve stories, values, and experiences unique to Jewish life. They connect generations through visual storytelling. They navigate the intersections of Jewish identity, intertwining faith, history, and cultural diversity in vivid and tangible ways. Moreover, they offer contemporary perspectives, exploring themes that resonate with modern Jewish experiences, from immigration to social justice.

Practices Today

- **Diverse Themes**: Artists explore many themes, including Jewish history, spirituality, and the Jewish diaspora, breathing fresh life into traditional forms.

- **Global Influence**: Jewish artists worldwide draw from their unique cultural contexts, infusing their works with global perspectives.
- **Cultural Dialogues:** These artworks often engage in dialogues with other artistic disciplines, promoting cross-cultural exchange and enriching the artistic landscape.
- **Community Engagement:** Exhibitions and collaborations within the Jewish community foster a sense of unity and shared cultural pride.

Jewish painting and sculpture can encapsulate the Jewish soul in art, inviting audiences of all backgrounds to explore the rich Jewish heritage and contemporary expression through the vibrant forms of the artistic realm.

Yiddish Theatre: The Heartbeat of Jewish Drama

Yiddish theatre, a vibrant and captivating cultural expression, has played a pivotal role in preserving and sharing Jewish stories, humor, and emotions.

Historical Context

Emerging in the late 19th century, Yiddish theatre took root in Jewish communities worldwide. It was a response to the challenges and triumphs of Jewish life, drawing inspiration from the Yiddish language and culture. These theatres became hubs of creativity and cultural exchange, with performances ranging from poignant dramas to uproarious comedies.

Cultural Significance

Yiddish theatre acted as a guardian of Yiddishkeit to preserve the Yiddish language and Jewish traditions through compelling narratives, reflecting the full spectrum of Jewish life; it depicted the struggles and dreams of Jewish communities. Moreover, it fostered a sense of unity among Jewish communities worldwide, transcending geographical and linguistic barriers.

Practices Today

- **Revival:** Yiddish theatre experiences a revival, with new generations embracing this art form and its linguistic and cultural roots.

- **Global Reach:** Productions now span the globe, bringing Yiddish stories to diverse audiences.
- **Interdisciplinary Collaborations:** Yiddish theatre often collaborates with other artistic disciplines, infusing new creativity into traditional narratives.
- **Cultural Festivals:** Festivals celebrate Yiddish theatre, promoting cultural exchange and preserving its legacy.

Yiddish theatre evokes laughter, tears, and contemplation. It remains the heartbeat of Jewish drama, inviting audiences of all backgrounds to revel in the timeless stories and emotions of Jewish life.

Jewish Textiles and Weaving Arts: Threads of Tradition and Faith

Jewish textiles and weaving arts, a symphony of colors and patterns, intricately interlace tradition, faith, and culture by creating objects like tallitot and challah covers.

Historical Context

These artistic traditions date back centuries, woven into the fabric of Jewish life. The intricate designs and weaving techniques have been passed down through generations.

Cultural Significance

Jewish textiles and weaving arts hold deep cultural significance. They embody the essence of prayer and ritual. Tallitot serves as garments of prayer that envelop the wearer in a sense of holiness during worship. Challah covers adorn the Shabbat table, elevating the sacred act of breaking bread. The patterns and colors used often carry symbolic meanings. Creating these textiles fosters bonds within families and communities as generations collaborate to produce these cherished pieces.

Practices Today

- **Contemporary Designs:** Artists infuse modern creativity into traditional weaving techniques, creating vibrant, contemporary designs.
- **Global Inspiration:** Jewish artisans draw inspiration worldwide, creating pieces that reflect diverse Jewish experiences.
- **Celebrations and Milestones:** These textiles play a central role in lifecycle events, from B'nei Mitzvah to weddings, preserving

traditions while marking new beginnings.

- **Artistic Expression**: Some Jewish weavers use these arts as a form of self-expression, blending cultural and artistic influences.

With their intricate beauty and rich symbolism, Jewish textiles and weaving arts are more than mere fabrics. They are tangible expressions of Jewish faith and creativity and invite individuals of all backgrounds to touch and connect with the timeless threads of tradition that continue to bind the Jewish community together.

Jewish Ceramics and Pottery: Crafting Tradition and Connection

Jewish ceramics and pottery, shaped by ancient techniques and modern creativity, form vessels of tradition and a bridge to Jewish heritage.

Historical Context

These artisanal crafts have roots deep in Jewish history. From biblical times to today, ceramics and pottery have served both functional and decorative purposes in Jewish households, synagogues, and ceremonial practices.

Cultural Significance

Ceramics and pottery often produce ceremonial objects like Kiddush cups and Hanukkah menorahs. These items enhance the observance of Jewish holidays and rituals. Artisans infuse their work with artistic expression, bridging the gap between the sacred and the creative.

Practices Today

- **Innovative Designs**: Artisans experiment with innovative designs, adapting ancient techniques to create unique and visually striking pieces.
- **Cultural Revival:** The resurgence of interest in Jewish heritage has sparked a revival of traditional Jewish ceramics.
- **Lifecycle Events**: Ceramics and pottery play an integral role in Jewish lifecycle events, from wedding chalices to memorial plaques, preserving traditions and marking significant moments.
- **Artistic Community**: The Jewish ceramics and pottery community is a thriving space for artists to connect, learn, and evolve their craft.

With their functional elegance and cultural depth, Jewish ceramics and pottery provide tangible links to Jewish history and spirituality. They serve as vessels of tradition, enriching Jewish rituals and inspiring contemporary artistry. These clay creations beckon to individuals of all backgrounds, inviting them to appreciate the timeless beauty they embody.

Judaica: Crafting Spiritual Connections

Judaica, an exquisite ensemble of Jewish ritual objects, are tangible artifacts with profound spirituality, embodying Jewish faith and tradition.

Historical Context

These sacred artifacts carry a rich historical legacy that spans millennia, originating in ancient times. Over the ages, Jewish communities across the globe have refined the craftsmanship behind these objects.

Cultural Significance

Judaica encompasses a multitude of meanings within its elegant forms. It enhances spiritual experiences and serves as a conduit for artistic expression. Each piece, from menorahs to kiddush cups, is a fusion of aesthetics and tradition. Moreover, Judaica forges bonds across generations as cherished objects are passed down, preserving family and communal memories.

Practices Today

- **Modern Designs**: Artisans infuse modern designs into these timeless objects, breathing new life into ancient traditions.

- **Global Artistry:** Judaica artists draw inspiration from diverse Jewish communities worldwide, enriching their creations with a mosaic of cultural. influences

- **Lifecycle Events**: Judaica plays pivotal roles in Jewish life cycle events, marking milestones and safeguarding tradition.

- **Cultural Preservation:** By meticulously crafting Judaica, artisans contribute to preserving Jewish culture and heritage.

Judaica embodies the enduring connection between Jewish people and their faith. These ritual objects invite individuals of all backgrounds to embrace the profound spirituality and cultural richness they encapsulate.

Art and creativity are essential facets of Jewish culture. Through these creative crafts, generations of Jews have expressed their faith and identity. These vibrant art forms continue to captivate people to explore the timeless beauty of Jewish tradition. By connecting with these arts, you can identify with the enduring legacy of the Jewish people and embrace a deeper sense of spirituality.

Chapter 10: The Culture of the Jewish Diaspora

The Jewish Diaspora means Jews living all over the world. Wherever Jewish people went, they adapted to the local culture while keeping their traditions. This created a rich mix of Jewish culture in different countries, making Jewish life colorful and diverse. Even in different lands, Jewish people kept their identity strong, connecting their past with their present.

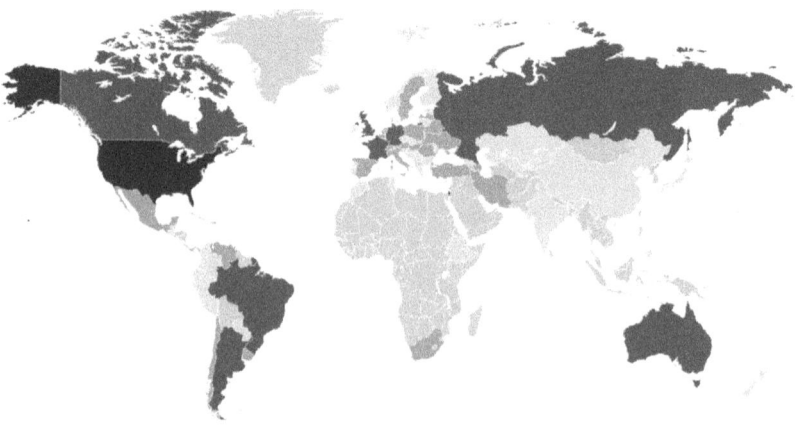

Map of the Jewish Diaspora.
Allice Hunter, CC BY-SA 4.0 <https://creativecommons.org/licenses/by-sa/4.0>, via Wikimedia Commons: https://commons.wikimedia.org/wiki/File:Map_of_the_Jewish_Diaspora_in_the_World.svg

The Diaspora's Impact on Jewish Culture and Traditions

The Jewish Diaspora has profoundly influenced Jewish culture and traditions, resulting in diverse geographical and cultural influences. This global journey has not diluted Jewish identity but, instead, has added layers of complexity and depth to Jewish life in countless ways.

- **Culinary Diversity:** Jewish cuisine has been deeply influenced by the regions where Jewish communities settled. In Eastern Europe, dishes like gefilte fish and matzah ball soup became staples, while Middle Eastern Jews brought flavors of falafel and hummus. Bagels became iconic in America. Each region's cuisine reflects Jewish dietary laws (kashrut) and local ingredients, creating a delectable blend of tradition and adaptation.

- **Musical Fusion:** Jewish music is a harmonious blend of various styles. Klezmer, a genre of Jewish folk music, thrived in Eastern Europe, while Mizrahi Jews introduced Middle Eastern melodies. In America, Jewish composers made significant contributions to classical and popular music. These influences created a rich musical mosaic that resonates with Jewish and non-Jewish audiences.

- **Linguistic Diversity:** Yiddish developed in Eastern Europe, combining Hebrew with local dialects. Ladino, a blend of Spanish and Hebrew, emerged among Sephardic Jews. These languages reflect Jewish communities' cultural and geographical roots.

- **Syncretic Traditions:** Jews adapted to their host cultures while preserving their religious practices. This syncretism created unique traditions, such as the Moroccan Jewish Mimouna celebration or the Bukharian Jewish wedding ceremony.

Sephardic Passover Customs: A Fusion of Tradition and Culture

Sephardic Passover customs exemplify the dynamic blend of timeless Jewish rituals and the diverse cultural influences of their diasporic communities.

Unique Cultural Practices

Sephardic Jews infuse their Passover traditions with regional flavors and customs:

- **Special Seder Plates:** These plates often feature unique items reflecting the Exodus story and local traditions. The roasted egg, intricately designed, mirrors the host country's culture.
- **Distinctive Passover Foods**: Sephardic cuisine incorporates local spices and ingredients, such as aromatic charoset, embodying the fusion of Jewish and regional flavors. Their matzah, thinner and pliable, echoes Mediterranean influences.

Customs

- **Ladino Haggadah:** Sephardic Jews may use a Ladino Haggadah, a Judeo-Spanish Passover text, connecting them to their Iberian roots.
- **Mimouna**: North African Jews celebrate Mimouna, a festive end to Passover. It features symbolic foods like flour and honey, embodying prosperity and fertility.
- **Kitniyot:** Sephardic Jews embrace kitniyot (legumes) on Passover, contrasting Ashkenazi traditions. This reflects Mediterranean and Middle Eastern culinary customs.

Adaptation and Fusion

Sephardic Passover customs demonstrate the adaptability of Jewish traditions in diverse settings. As they migrated and coexisted with other cultures, Sephardic Jews retained the essence of Passover while enriching their customs with local influences.

Ashkenazi Klezmer Music: A Harmonious Blend of Cultures

Ashkenazi Klezmer music is a testament to the harmonious fusion of Jewish musical traditions and the vibrant tapestry of the Ashkenazi Jewish diaspora.

Unique Cultural Practices

Ashkenazi Klezmer music showcases a distinct blend of Jewish and Eastern European influences:

- **Instrumentation:** Traditional Klezmer ensembles feature clarinets, violins, and accordions, reflecting the instrumental diversity of Eastern European folk music.

- **Diverse Melodies**: The music incorporates a range of emotions, from joyous dances like the "Hora" to soulful melodies conveying the Jewish spirit of resilience.

Customs

Klezmer music carries with it customs that mirror the Ashkenazi Jewish experience:

- **Wedding Celebrations**: Klezmer music has been integral to Ashkenazi Jewish weddings for centuries, enhancing the festive atmosphere with lively tunes.
- **Simchas**: It's also an essential element of joyous celebrations, known as "simchas," which include bar and bat mitzvahs and other communal events.

Adaptation and Blending

Ashkenazi Klezmer's music beautifully illustrates the adaptability of Jewish traditions in diverse locales. As Ashkenazi Jews settled in Eastern Europe, their music absorbed their host countries' melodies, rhythms, and scales, resulting in a distinctive Klezmer sound that resonates with Jewish heritage and European influences. This musical genre epitomizes the ability of Jewish culture to flourish and evolve in the diaspora, leaving an indelible mark on the world's musical tapestry.

Mizrahi Jewish Cuisine: A Feast of Diverse Heritage

Mizrahi Jewish cuisine, a culinary treasure trove, offers a delectable testament to the fusion of Jewish culinary traditions with the rich Middle East and North Africa tapestry.

Unique Cultural Practices

- **Spices and Flavors**: It features an array of aromatic spices and bold flavors characteristic of Middle Eastern and North African cuisine.
- **Festive Dishes**: Mizrahi Jews celebrate holidays and milestones with unique dishes, such as fragrant rice dishes like "*Makloubeh*" for special occasions.

Customs
- **Shabbat Meals**: Lavish Shabbat feasts often include dishes like "*chraime*," a spicy fish stew, reflecting the fusion of culinary traditions and religious observance.
- **Passover Seder**: Unique Passover dishes like "*kibbeh*," bulgur wheat meatballs, add a distinct flavor to the holiday celebration.

Adaptation and Blending

Mizrahi Jewish cuisine beautifully illustrates the adaptability of Jewish culinary traditions. As Mizrahi Jews settled in the Middle East and North Africa, they embraced local ingredients and techniques, infusing their cuisine with a rich array of regional spices and flavors. This culinary fusion is a testament to the resilience and creativity of Jewish communities in adapting and thriving in diverse diasporic settings.

Beta Israel (Ethiopian Jewish) Sigd Festival: A Celebration of Faith and Community

The Beta Israel, or *Ethiopian Jewish Sigd Festival*, is a unique and vibrant celebration that encapsulates the spiritual journey of a community bound by faith and a longing for Jerusalem.

Unique Cultural Practices
- **Mountain Ascent**: Beta Israel members gather on high mountains, emulating the biblical ascent to Mount Sinai, where they receive the Ten Commandments.
- **Prayers and Fasting**: Prayers, Psalms, and communal fasting are central to the Sigd as the community renews its commitment to the Torah.

Customs
- **White Attire**: Participants wear traditional white garments, symbolizing purity and spiritual renewal.
- **Torah Scrolls**: The Torah scrolls are central to the celebration, highlighting the enduring connection to Jewish traditions.

Adaptation and Resilience

The Sigd Festival reflects Beta Israel's unwavering faith and resilience throughout history. While separated from global Jewish communities for centuries, they preserved their Jewish identity and traditions. The Sigd Festival, celebrated today in Israel, is a remarkable testament to their enduring spirit and reconnection with the broader Jewish world. It is a joyous reminder that faith transcends time and distance, uniting the Beta Israel with their Jewish heritage.

Bnei Menashe (India) Shabbat Observances: Honoring the Sabbath in the Hills of Northeast India

Shabbat observance among the Bnei Menashe, a Jewish community in India's northeastern hills, is a unique fusion of traditional Jewish customs and the rich cultural tapestry of their Indian homeland.

Unique Cultural Practices

Bnei Menashe Shabbat observances are typically a blend of Jewish traditions together with regional customs:

- **Community Gatherings:** Families and neighbors come together for communal Shabbat meals, fostering a sense of unity and solidarity.
- **Traditional Indian Flavors:** Shabbat meals feature Indian dishes infused with local spices, offering a culinary celebration that resonates with the region's rich flavors.

Customs

- **Candle Lighting:** Lighting Shabbat candles is a cherished tradition, signifying the beginning of the holy day and evoking a sense of spirituality.
- **Songs and Prayers:** The Bnei Menashe engage in songs and prayers that blend Hebrew and their native languages, creating a unique musical and spiritual experience.

Adaptation and Integration

Shabbat observances among the Bnei Menashe exemplify the community's ability to maintain Jewish traditions while integrating local customs. Their Shabbat customs evolved as they journeyed to Israel, intertwining with the broader Jewish traditions. Yet, their observance remains deeply rooted in the unique cultural and culinary traditions of their Indian homeland, showcasing their adaptability and the enduring importance of Shabbat in their lives.

Yemenite Jewish Art and Poetry: A Timeless Expression of Faith and Culture

The art and poetry of Yemenite Jews offer a captivating window into a rich and ancient Jewish tradition deeply entwined with Yemeni culture.

Unique Cultural Practices

- **Illuminated Manuscripts**: Yemenite Jewish scribes created stunning illuminated manuscripts of sacred texts, blending meticulous calligraphy with vibrant geometric designs.

- **Qasidah Poetry:** Yemenite Jews have a long tradition of composing qasidahs, Arabic poems that celebrate religious themes and express devotion to God.

Customs

- **Synagogue Decorations**: Elaborate artistry adorns Yemenite synagogues, from intricately designed Torah arks to colorful mosaic floors.

- **Liturgical Poetry:** Qasidahs are sung during religious rituals, enhancing the spiritual experience and connecting the community to its poetic heritage.

Adaptation and Preservation

- **Preservation of Manuscripts**: Despite their diaspora, Yemenite Jews have diligently preserved their illuminated manuscripts, safeguarding their cultural and religious heritage.

- **Continued Creation**: In Israel and other diaspora communities, Yemenite Jewish artists and poets continue to create works that honor their traditions while adapting to modern contexts.

Yemenite Jewish art and poetry are a testament to the enduring power of creativity and faith. These vibrant expressions of culture and spirituality enrich the tapestry of Jewish heritage, serving as a bridge between the past and the present.

Ladino (Judeo-Spanish) Language Revitalization: Preserving Sephardic Heritage through Words

The Ladino language, a precious linguistic gem, is undergoing a revival, breathing life into Sephardic Jewish heritage and connecting generations to their roots.

Unique Cultural Practices

The revitalization of Ladino is characterized by efforts to reclaim a language nearly lost to history:

- **Ladino Classes:** Communities worldwide offer Ladino language classes to reconnect with their heritage.
- **Digital Repositories:** Efforts to digitize Ladino texts and recordings ensure that the language remains accessible to future generations.

Customs

- **Ladino Music:** Ladino songs and music, with their poetic lyrics, serve as a cultural bridge that reinforces the language's importance.
- **Ladino Literature:** Literary works in Ladino, including folk tales and newspapers, are cherished for preserving Sephardic history and culture.

The revitalization of Ladino signifies more than just a linguistic revival. It's a vibrant celebration of a rich and diverse heritage. Through Ladino, Sephardic Jews honor their ancestors and forge a cultural legacy that transcends time and borders.

Bukharan Jewish Weddings: A Tapestry of Traditions and Celebrations

Bukharan Jewish weddings are a captivating blend of ancient traditions and vibrant celebrations, reflecting the rich cultural heritage of the Bukharan Jewish community.

Unique Cultural Practices

- **Henna Ceremony:** Before the wedding, the bride's hands and feet are adorned with intricate henna designs, symbolizing beauty and protection.

- **Matchmakers:** Matchmakers play a pivotal role in arranging marriages, emphasizing family connections and cultural compatibility.

Customs

- **Seven Blessings:** During the ceremony, seven blessings are recited, each emphasizing different aspects of love, joy, and companionship.
- **Crowning:** The bride and groom are crowned, symbolizing their roles as king and queen of their new life together.

Bukharan Jewish weddings are a beautiful tapestry of history, culture, and love. They showcase the enduring spirit of a community that has navigated through centuries of change while maintaining a deep connection to its roots.

Syrian Jewish Calligraphy and Weaving: Threads of Artistry and Devotion

The artistry of Syrian Jewish calligraphy and weaving is a testament to a community's enduring creativity and faith that has enriched Jewish culture for centuries.

Unique Cultural Practices

- **Hebrew Calligraphy:** Syrian Jewish scribes employ intricate Hebrew calligraphy, transforming sacred texts into visual works of art.
- **Silk Weaving:** Syrian Jewish artisans are renowned for their silk weaving, creating vibrant textiles that reflect the colors and patterns of the region.

Customs

- **Torah Scrolls:** Elaborate Hebrew calligraphy adorns Torah scrolls, imbuing these sacred texts with artistic beauty and spiritual significance.
- **Tallis:** Handwoven silk tallitot are cherished family heirlooms passed down through generations and worn during prayer.

Syrian Jewish calligraphy and weaving exemplify the enduring legacy of a community that seamlessly merges artistic excellence with religious devotion.

Persian Jewish Poetry and Music: Echoes of a Timeless Culture

Persian Jewish poetry and music form an exquisite tapestry that reflects the deep cultural and spiritual connections of a community that has flourished for centuries in the heart of Iran.

Unique Cultural Practices

- **Persian Poetry:** Persian Jewish poets have contributed to the rich tradition of Persian poetry, weaving themes of love, longing, and spirituality.
- **Musical Instruments:** Traditional Persian instruments like the tar and setar uniquely flavor Persian Jewish musical compositions.

Customs

- **Shabbat Songs:** Persian Jewish communities have their repertoire of Shabbat songs, combining Hebrew and Persian melodies.
- **Poetic Prayer:** Persian Jewish liturgy often includes poetic prayers, adding emotional depth to religious observance.

Persian Jewish poetry and music are poignant expressions of a community's resilience and devotion. These creative traditions serve as bridges connecting the past, present, and future, ensuring that the rich tapestry of Persian Jewish culture remains vibrant and enduring.

The Jewish diaspora comprises many distinct cultures that share a common heritage. From Ladino to Persian Jewish poetry, the vibrant traditions of the world's Jewish communities are living legacies that honor their ancestors while inspiring future generations. Through artistry and faith, these timeless customs will continue to enrich Jewish culture for centuries. By preserving and celebrating these vibrant expressions of culture, Jews honor their ancestors and connect to a larger global Jewish community.

Conclusion

Judaism, one of the world's oldest monotheistic religions, has evolved significantly since its early inception, shaped by historical events, migrations, and interactions with other cultures and religions. This evolution has resulted in the diverse tapestry of Jewish traditions seen today.

Historical Evolution

- **Biblical Era:** In its early days, Judaism was centered around temple worship in Jerusalem, focusing on animal sacrifices and strict adherence to Mosaic law as outlined in the Torah. The Exodus and the giving of the Ten Commandments were foundational events.

- **Diaspora:** The Jewish Diaspora marked a pivotal shift, beginning with the Babylonian exile. Jews dispersed worldwide, adapting to their host countries' cultures while maintaining their religious identity. This dispersion fostered syncretism and the development of distinct traditions in various regions.

- **Rabbinic Judaism:** After the destruction of the Second Temple in 70 CE, Rabbinic Judaism emerged. It emphasized the authority of rabbis, the study of the Talmud, and the importance of synagogues and home-based religious practices. Rabbinic Judaism became the dominant form of Judaism.

Notable and Popular Traditions Today

- **Sabbath (Shabbat):** The observance of Shabbat from Friday evening to Saturday evening remains a cornerstone of Jewish life, marked by lighting candles, reciting blessings, and enjoying festive meals.
- **Passover (Pesach):** The Passover Seder, with its symbolic foods and retelling of the Exodus, is widely observed, even by secular Jews.
- **Hanukkah:** The lighting of the menorah and the exchange of gifts during Hanukkah continue to be popular and widely recognized Jewish customs.

Less Common Traditions

- **Pilgrimage to Jerusalem:** While visiting Jerusalem remains significant, the concept of pilgrimage to the Temple, a central practice in ancient times, is no longer observed due to the absence of the Temple.
- **Animal Sacrifice:** Animal sacrifice, a fundamental aspect of early Judaism, ceased with the destruction of the Second Temple and the shift to Rabbinic Judaism.

Influences and Crossroads with Other Religions

- **Influence on Christianity:** Christianity, which emerged from a Jewish context, adopted elements of Jewish tradition, such as the Hebrew Bible (Old Testament) and the monotheistic belief in one God. However, it also diverged significantly in theological interpretations and practices, notably the role of Jesus as the Messiah.
- **Influence on Islam:** Islam shares some commonalities with Judaism, including belief in one God and reverence for many biblical figures. The Quran recognizes the People of the Book, which includes Jews, emphasizing common religious roots.
- **Influence on Buddhism:** Some scholars suggest that Jewish communities in India might have influenced early Buddhist thought. The concept of suffering and liberation from it bears resemblance to Jewish themes.

- **Influence of Other Religions on Judaism:** Throughout history, Judaism has absorbed elements from other cultures and religions in the lands where Jews settled. This syncretism enriched Jewish traditions, leading to practices like Mimouna (North African Jewish celebration) and Bukharian Jewish customs.

Judaism's evolution has been marked by adaptation, resilience, and a dynamic interplay with other religions and cultures. Today, it stands as a diverse and vibrant faith with a rich tapestry of traditions that reflect the historical journey of the Jewish people. While some practices have faded into history, others remain integral to contemporary Jewish life, offering a unique blend of continuity and adaptation that defines Judaism in the modern world.

Glossary of Terms

An A - Z glossary of terms for various Jewish traditions, along with their pronunciation and English translations:

- **Amidah (ah-MEE-dah)** - The central Jewish prayer recited while standing, also known as the Shemoneh Esrei
- **Ashkenazi (ahsh-keh-NAH-zee)** - Jews of Eastern European descent, known for their Klezmer music
- **Bar Mitzvah (bar meetz-VAH)** - A Jewish boy's coming-of-age ceremony at age thirteen
- **Bat Mitzvah (baht meetz-VAH)** - A Jewish girl's coming-of-age ceremony at age twelve or thirteen
- **Birkat HaMazon (beer-KAHT hah-MAH-zohn)** - The grace recited after meals, thanking God
- **Bnei Menashe (buh-NAY Muh-NAH-she)** - A group in India and Myanmar with unique Shabbat observances
- **Brit Milah (breet mee-LAH)** - The Jewish circumcision ceremony
- **Challah (HAH-lah)** - Braided bread traditionally eaten on Shabbat
- **Chuppah (khoo-PAH)** - A wedding canopy symbolizing the home the couple will build
- **Dreidel (DRAY-dul)** - A spinning top used during the Hanukkah game

- **Eicha (ay-KHAH)** - The Book of Lamentations, read on Tisha B'Av
- **Haftarah (hahf-tah-RAH)** - A selection from the Prophets read after the Torah portion
- **Hanukkah (HAH-noo-kah)** - The Festival of Lights commemorates the miracle of the oil
- **Hazzanut (hah-zah-NOOT)** - The art of cantorial music, performed by cantors (hazzans)
- **Kaddish (KAH-dish)** - A prayer recited in memory of the deceased
- **Ketubah (keh-TOO-bah)** - A Jewish marriage contract
- **Kiddush (kee-DOOSH)** - A blessing over wine, sanctifying Shabbat
- **Klezmer (KLEZ-muhr)** - Traditional Ashkenazi Jewish instrumental music is often associated with celebrations
- **Kol Nidre (kohl NEE-dray)** - A special prayer service on the eve of Yom Kippur
- **Lulav and Etrog (LOO-lahv and ET-rog)** - Plants used in the rituals of Sukkot
- **Matzah (MAHT-suh)** - Unleavened bread eaten during Passover
- **Mezuzah (meh-ZOO-zah)** - A parchment inscribed with Torah verses affixed to the doorposts of Jewish homes
- **Menorah (muh-NOH-ruh)** - A seven-branched candelabrum, often associated with the Temple in Jerusalem
- **Midrash (MID-rash)** - Rabbinic interpretations and elaborations on biblical texts
- **Mizrahi (miz-RAH-hee)** - Jews of Middle Eastern and North African descent with diverse culinary traditions
- **Mohel (MOH-huhl)** - The person trained to perform circumcisions
- **Ne'ila (nay-EE-luh)** - The closing service of Yom Kippur
- **Pizmonim (PEEZ-moh-neem)** - Traditional Sephardic songs often sung during festive occasions

- **Purim (POO-reem)** - A joyous holiday celebrating the story of Esther
- **Rosh Hashanah (ROHSH hah-shuh-NAH)** - The Jewish New Year
- **Seder (SAY-duhr)** - The ritual meal and ceremony on the first two nights of Passover
- **Shabbat (SHA-baht)** - The Jewish Sabbath, observed from Friday evening to Saturday evening
- **Shema (SHEH-mah)** - The central Jewish declaration of faith found in the Torah (Deuteronomy 6:4)
- **Sheva Brachot (SHEH-vuh BRAH-kot)** - Seven blessings recited during a Jewish wedding ceremony
- **Shiva (SHEE-vuh)** - A period of mourning for seven days after the burial of a close relative
- **Shofar (shoh-FAHR)** - A ram's horn blown on certain Jewish holidays
- **Sukkah (SOO-kah)** - A temporary hut or booth constructed for the holiday of Sukkot
- **Sukkot (SOO-kawt)** - The Feast of Tabernacles or Booths
- **Synagogue (SIN-uh-gahg)** - A Jewish place of worship, often with distinct architectural features
- **Tallit (TAH-lit)** - A prayer shawl with fringes (tzitzit) worn during prayer
- **Tashlich (TAHSH-leekh)** - A ritual symbolically casting away sins into a body of water
- **Tefillin (teh-FIL-in)** - Small black boxes containing verses from the Torah, worn during weekday morning prayers
- **Tisha B'Av (TEE-shah BAHV)** - The fast day mourning the destruction of the First and Second Temples
- **Torah (TOH-ruh)** - The central and most sacred text of Judaism, comprising the first five books of the Bible
- **Tu B'Shevat (too b'shuh-VAHT)** - The Jewish holiday celebrating the New Year for Trees, often observed with a Seder

- **Yahrzeit (YAHR-zate)** - The anniversary of a loved one's death
- **Yizkor (yiz-KOHR)** - A memorial service held on certain holidays
- **Yom Kippur (YOHM kip-POOR)** - The Day of Atonement, observed with a 25-hour fast

References

(N.d.). Com.au. https://culturalatlas.sbs.com.au/religions/judaism/resources/judaism-rituals-and-practices

How to host the best Shabbat dinner party — My Jewish Life magazine. (n.d.). Googleadservices.com. https://myjewishmommylife.com/2019/09/10/how-to-host-an-elegant-dinner-party-for-shabbat/Jewish custom. (n.d.). Judaism. https://www.keralatourism.org/judaism/life/jewish-custom

Jewish holidays & celebrations explained. (2017, November 5). Peninsula Jewish Community Center. https://pjcc.org/jewish-life/jewish-holidays-explained/

Jewish traditions explained. (2018, October 5). JConnect; Jconnet. https://www.jconnect.org/resources/jewish-traditions-explained/

Mitchell, T. (2016, March 8). 5. Jewish beliefs and practices. Pew Research Center's Religion & Public Life Project. https://www.pewresearch.org/religion/2016/03/08/jewish-beliefs-and-practices/

Mitchell, T. (2021, May 11). 3. Jewish practices and customs. Pew Research Center's Religion & Public Life Project. https://www.pewresearch.org/religion/2021/05/11/jewish-practices-and-customs/

Novak, D., Greenberg, M., Pines, S., Silberman, L. H., Dimitrovsky, H. Z., Vajda, G., Hertzberg, A., Cohen, G. D., Gaster, T. H., Feldman, L. H., & Baron, S. W. (2023). Judaism. In Encyclopedia Britannica.

Prague City Line » Jewish traditions and customs. (n.d.). Praguecityline.com. https://www.praguecityline.com/jewish-prague/jewish-traditions-and-customs

www.ingramcontent.com/pod-product-compliance
Lightning Source LLC
Chambersburg PA
CBHW070330010526
44107CB00004B/485